James M. Black

Chorus of Praise

James M. Black

Chorus of Praise

ISBN/EAN: 9783337334345

Printed in Europe, USA, Canada, Australia, Japan

Cover: Foto ©Thomas Meinert / pixelio.de

More available books at **www.hansebooks.com**

—THE— CHORUS OF PRAISE

FOR USE IN

Sunday Schools, Young People's Meetings,

Revivals, Prayer Meetings,

AND

All the Social Services of the Church.

EDITED BY

J. M. BLACK.

"Let all the people sing."

EATON & MAINS,
New York, Boston, Pittsburg, Detroit, San Francisco.

CURTS & JENNINGS,
Cincinnati, Chicago, St. Louis.

Copyright, 1898, by Eaton & Mains.

CONTENTS.

Title	No.
Abide With Me	67
A Charge to Keep	143
A Light that is	64
Am I a Soldier	134
And can I yet	144
Anywhere with Jesus	10
Anywhere with Jesus is	41
Arise my Soul	139
Awake and Sing	121
Beautiful Eden Bells	19
Beautiful Robes	62
Be Ready when	5
Blessed Assurance	74
Blest be the Tie	142
By and By	40
Calvary	34
Come Home to-night	36
Come my Soul	116
Come Sound His	119
Come to Him Now	77
Come ye Disconsolate	146
Come ye Sinners	131
Down low at my	3
Forever here my Rest	135
Glory to His Name	95
God Be With You	89
Gracious Spirit	118
Guide Me, Great	155
Hasten Sinner	123
Hear the Word	2
Heavenly Father	81
Heaven's Harvest	50
He Hideth my Soul	35
He is Mine, I am	58
Help me Master	51
He's Coming By and	18
He Save Me	20
His Wondrous Love	53
How Firm a Foundation	111
How Sweet the Name	136
I Love Thy Kingdom	153
I love to Tell	104
I'll Go where you	106
I'll Live for Him	109
I must Tell Jesus	13
I'm Going Home	128
I Need Thee	85
I Never will Cease to	75
In the Cross	126
I Shall be like	15
It was Spoken	94
Jesus, I Come	105
Jesus is Good to Me	45
Jesus is Passing	102
Jesus is Pleading	31
Jesus Lover of My Soul	140
Jesus, Saviour, Pilot Me	69
Jesus Thine all	151
Jesus the Light	91
Jesus will Care	63
Jesus your only	29
Joy to the World	124
Just as I Am	112
Just the same	108
Lead Me Saviour	17
Leaning on the	49
Let Him In	101
Let the Blessed Saviour	52
Lives of Purpose	33
Looking this Way	25
Marching to Zion	130
Meet Me There	54
More than Life to	14
Mourn for the	145
My Country 'tis of	127
My Faith Looks up to	114
My Jesus as Thou	129
My Jesus I Love	137
My Lord and King	47
My Saviour First	26
My Saviour is with	46
My Spirit on Thy	120
Nearer My God	59
Nearer to our Saviour	11
Neither Do I Condemn	42
No, Not One	107
O Blessed Holy Spirit	44
O could I Speak	152
O for a Faith	133
O for a Heart	132
On the Way	79
O what Amazing	149
Pass Me Not	37
Praise God	158
Revive Thy Work	141
Revive us Again	154
Saviour, Blessed Saviour	66
Scattering Precious	99
Seeking for Me	72
Serving Jesus	39
Since the Love of	27
Since Jesus my Saviour	60
Sitting at the Feet	43
Stand Up for Jesus	156
Stepping in the Light	71
Step Out on the	97
Some Happy Day	16
Songs of Praise	122
Sunlight all the Way	92
Sunshine as you Go	6
Take my Life and	115
Tell Me once more	32
Tell the Sweet	88
The Beautiful Light	56
The best Friend	68
The Bolted Door	28
The Call for Reapers	93
The Christ who died	21
The Comforter has Come	8
The Friendship of	61
The Master is Come	30
The morning Light	157
The Saviour for You	82
The Spirit and the	12
The way of the	103
There'll be no Dark	48
There is a Fountain	113
There's a great Day	100
There's a Wideness	138
They who Seek	117
Thou Thinkest Lord	83
Thy Boundless Love	7
To Jesus Draw Nigh	24
Twilight	110
Unto You is	98
Walking in the Way	4
Walk in the Light	148
Walking With Him	9
Watch and Pray	87
We'll Never Say Good	65
What a Friend	55
What a Gathering	96
What a Wonderful	22
When I survey	147
When all thy Mercies	150
When the King	84
When the Roll	80
When the Saints	57
Where He Leads	76
Where Jesus is	1
Whiter than Snow	38
Whosoever that	78
Wilt Thou be made	90
Will you Give all	70
Witness for Jesus	23
Wonderful piece	73
Wonderful Story of	86
Work for the Night	125

THE
Chorus of Praise

No. 1.   Where Jesus is, 'Tis Heaven.

C. F. BUTLER.   J. M. BLACK.

1. Since Christ my soul from sin set free, This world has been a heav'n to me;
2. Once heav-en seemed a far-off place, Till Je-sus showed His smiling face;
3. What mat-ters where on earth we dwell? On mountain top, or in the dell?

And, 'mid earth's sorrows and its woe, 'Tis heav'n my Je-sus here to know.
Now it's be-gun with-in my soul, 'Twill last while endless a-ges roll.
In cot-tage, or a man-sion fair, Where Je-sus is, 'tis heav-en there.

CHORUS.

O hal-le-lu-jah, yes 'tis heav'n, 'Tis heav'n to know my sins forgiv'n;

On land or sea, what matters where, Where Jesus is, 'tis heav-en there.

Copyright, 1898, by J. M. Black.

No. 4. Walking in the Way with Jesus.

LIDA M. KECK.
J. M. BLACK.

1. While walk-ing in the way with Je-sus, Se-cure from ev - 'ry storm that blows, I'm kept in per-fect peace from all my foes, While
2. While walk-ing in the way with Je-sus, I bid fare-well to all my fears, A bow of prom-ise glows a-bove my tears, While
3. While walk-ing in the way with Je-sus, I hear His "Come to Me and rest," And, look-ing un-to Him, my soul is blest While
4. While walk-ing in the way with Je-sus, I see my heav'n-ly home a-far; I see the pearl-y gates for me a-jar, While

walk-ing in the way with Je-sus.

CHORUS.

Walk-ing in the way with Je-sus, Walk-ing in the way with Je-sus, I'm kept in perfect peace, My joys in-crease, While walk-ing in the way with Je-sus.

Copyright, 1898, by J. M. Black.

No. 9. Walking With Him To-Day.

B. M. J.
J. M. BLACK.

1. Lean-ing on Je-sus, can aught be-tide me? Walking with Him,
2. Shad-ows de-part and the way grows bright-er, Walking with Him,
3. He is my guide and the way He know-eth, Walking with Him,

walk-ing with Him; He will de-liv-er, pro-tect and guide me,
walk-ing with Him; Tri-als are few-er and bur-dens light-er,
walk-ing with Him; Peace like a riv-er my soul o'er-flow-eth,

CHORUS.

Walk-ing with Him to-day. Walking and talk-ing with my dear Sav-iour, Com-fort and bless-ings a-bound in my way; O, I re-joice in His great sal-va-tion, Walking with Him to-day.

Copyright, 1893, by Chas. H. Gabriel.

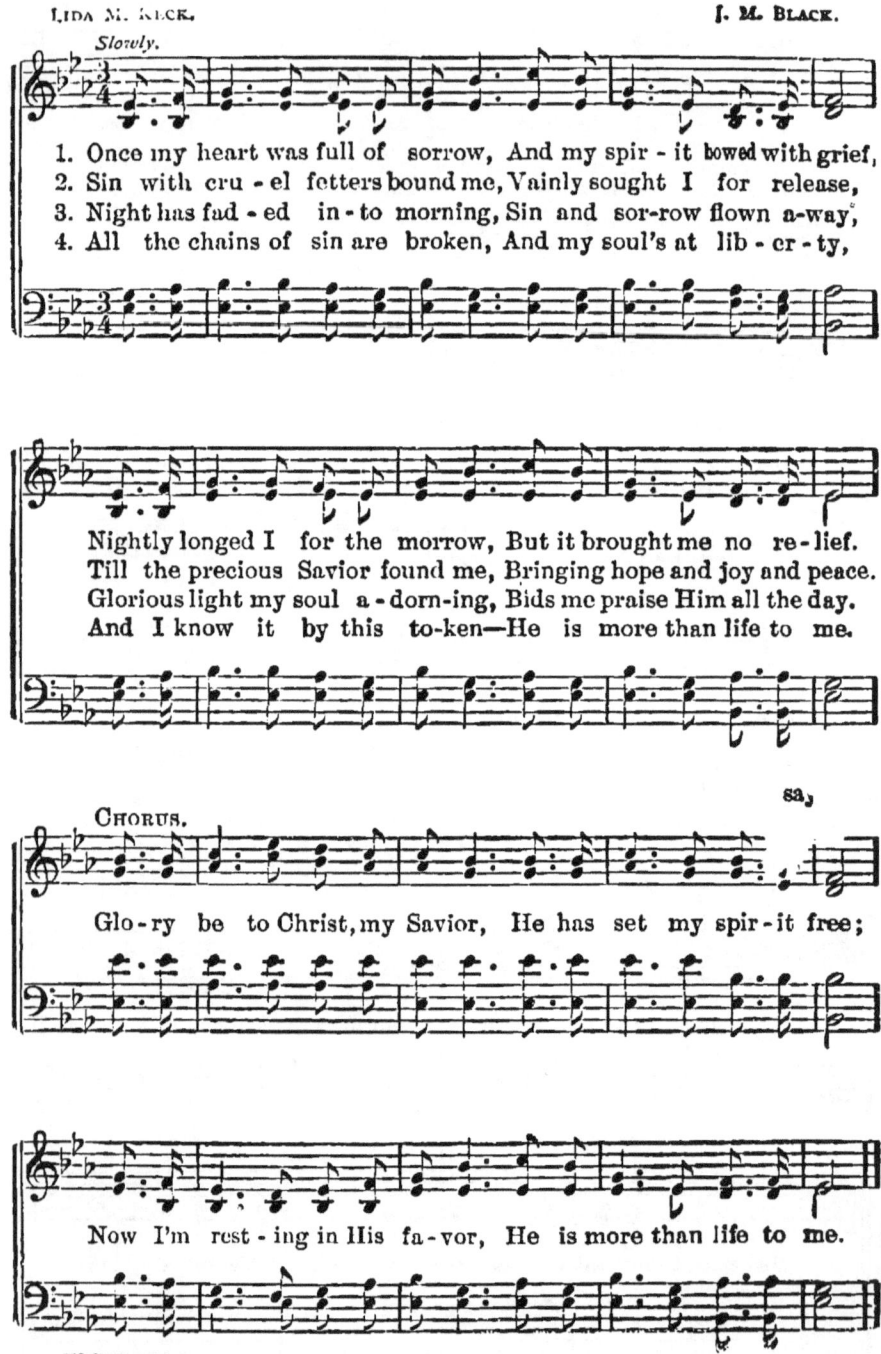

No. 18. He's Coming By and By.

LIZZIE AKERS.   J. M. BLACK.

1. The bells of hope ring in my soul, And, oh, how sweet their chime!
2. It may be at the e-ven-tide, My Lord will come for me,
3. So, watch-ing, pray-ing, toil-ing on, Still cheered by hope's sweet bells,

Their song keeps ring-ing day by day Thro' bus-y work-ing time.
Or that the si-lent mid-night hour His chos-en time will be.
I jour-ney to the Beu-lah land Where joy for-ev-er dwells.

Tho' wea-ry oft with toil and care, Tho' oft for rest I sigh,
He gent-ly bids me watch and wait; When un-to Him I cry,
I catch a glimpse of Ca-naan's shore, My home be-yond the sky,

Hope's bells my faint-ing spir-it cheer, He's com-ing by and by.
And tunes my heart to hope's re-frain, He's com-ing by and by.
All glo-ry to His precious name! He's com-ing by and by.

REFRAIN.

He's com-ing by and by, He's com-ing by and by.

Copyright, 1898, by J. M. Black.

He's Coming By and By.—Concluded.

The bells of hope ring in my soul, He's com-ing by and by.

No. 19. Beautiful Eden Bells.

FANNY J. CROSBY.   J. M. BLACK.

1. Beau-ti-ful bells of E-den fair, Chiming at eve on the calm, still air,
2. Beau-ti-ful bells of E-den bright, Murmuring on thro' the hush of night,
3. Beau-ti-ful bells of E-den chime, Softly they breathe in their tones sublime;

Lift-ing the soul with its toil oppress'd, Into the vales of the pure and bless'd.
Tell-ing my soul of the friends I love, Gather'd and safe in their home above.
Ech-o of joy from a white-robed throng, Praising the Lord in a world of song.

CHORUS.   *rit.*

Sweet, beauti-ful bells; . . . That oft in a dream I hear. . . .
so dear;   in a dream I hear,

rit. ad lib.

Welcome the message they bring to me, O-ver the waves of the crys-tal sea.

Copyright 1898 by J. M. Black.

No. 22. What a Wonderful Saviour!

"And His name shall be called Wonderful."—Isa. 9: 6.

E. A. H. ELISHA A. HOFFMANN.

1. Christ has for sin a-tonement made, What a wonderful Saviour! We are redeemed! the price is paid! What a wonderful Saviour!
2. I praise Him for the cleansing blood, What a wonderful Saviour! That rec-on-ciled my soul to God; What a wonderful Saviour!
3. He cleansed my heart from all its sin, What a wonderful Saviour! And now He reigns and rules therein; What a wonderful Saviour!
4. He walks be-side me in the way, What a wonderful Saviour! And keeps me faithful day by day; What a wonderful Saviour!

CHORUS.
What a wonderful Saviour is Jesus, my Jesus!
What a wonderful Saviour is Jesus, my Lord!

5 He gives me overcoming power,
   What a wonderful Saviour!
   And triumph in each trying hour;
   What a wonderful Saviour!

6 To Him I've given all my heart,
   What a wonderful Saviour!
   The world shall never share a part;
   What a wonderful Saviour!

Copyright, 1891, by The Biglow & Main Co., used by per.

No. 26. My Saviour First of All.

FANNY J. CROSBY.   JNO. R. SWENEY.

1. When my life-work is ended, and I cross the swelling tide, When the bright and glorious morning I shall see; I shall know my Redeemer when I reach the other side, And His smile will be the first to welcome me.
2. Oh, the soul-thrilling rapture when I view His blessed face, And the lustre of His kindly beaming eye; How my full heart will praise Him for the mercy, love, and grace, That prepares for me a mansion in the sky.
3. Oh, the dear ones is glory, how they beckon me to come, And our parting at the river I recall; To the sweet vales of Eden they will sing my welcome home; But I long to meet my Saviour first of all.
4. Thro' the gates to the city in a robe of spotless white, He will lead me where no tears will ever fall; In the glad song of ages I shall mingle with delight; But I long to meet my Saviour first of all.

CHORUS.
I shall know Him, I shall know Him, And redeemed by His side I shall stand;
I shall know Him, I shall know Him By the print of the nails in His hand.

Copyright, 1891 by Jno R. Sweney. Used by per.

No. 30.   The Master is Come.

"The Master is come and calleth for thee." John, 11: 28

KATHARINE E. PURVIS.   J. M. BLACK.

1. "The Mas-ter is come," O pen-i-tent one, He brings thee for-giveness and love; The cup that He drain'd thy par-don has won—
2. "The Mas-ter is come," O la-bor-er know The seed thou art sow-ing in tears, Thro' sunshine and storm shall blossom and grow
3. "The Mas-ter is come," O pilgrim, whose way Has lain in the shad-ow so long, Thy path will lead home to por-tals of day—
4. "The Mas-ter is come," O mourn-er re-joice, He robs e-ven death of its sting; Thy lov'd shall a-wake at sound of His voice

Thy ti-tle to mansions a-bove.
To ri-pen in heaven's bright years.
To joy and redemption's glad song.
To dwell ev-er-more with the King.

CHORUS.

"The Mas-ter is come and call-eth for thee," O soul heav-y la-den, op-pressed, He call-eth for thee, He calleth for thee, Draw near unto Him and find rest.

COPYRIGHT 1907, BY J. M. BLACK.

No. 34. Calvary.

"The place which is called Calvary, there they crucified Him."—LUKE 23:33.

Rev. W. M'K. DARWOOD. JNO. R. SWENEY.

1. On Calv'ry's brow......... my Saviour died,......... 'Twas there my Lord......... was cru-ci-fied:......... 'Twas on the cross......... He bled for me,......... And purchased there......... my par-don free.
2. 'Mid rending rocks......... and dark'ning skies,......... My Saviour bows......... His head and dies;......... The opening vail......... reveals the way......... To heaven's joys......... and end-less day.
3. O Je-sus, Lord,......... how can it be,......... That Thou shouldst give......... Thy life for me,......... To bear the cross......... and ag-o-ny,—......... In that dread hour......... on Cal-va-ry!

CHORUS.

O Cal-va-ry! dark Cal-va-ry! Where Jesus shed His blood for me, for me;
O Cal-va-ry! blest Cal-va-ry! 'Twas there my Sav-iour died for me.

Copyright, 1886, by Jno. R. Sweney. Used by per.

No. 35. He Hideth My Soul.

FANNY J. CROSBY. WM. J. KIRKPATRICK.
Allegretto.

1. A won-der-ful Sav-iour is Je-sus my Lord, A won-der-ful Sav-iour to me, He hid-eth my soul in the cleft of the rock, Where riv-ers of pleasure I see.
2. A won-der-ful Sav-iour is Je-sus my Lord, He tak-eth my bur-den a-way, He hold-eth me up, and I shall not be moved, He giv-eth me strength as my day.
3. With num-ber-less blessings each mo-ment He crowns, And fill'd with His full-ness di-vine, I sing in my rapt-ure, oh, glo-ry to God For such a Redeemer as mine.
4. When clothed in His brightness transported I rise To meet Him in clouds of the sky, His per-fect sal-va-tion, His won-der-ful love, I'll shout with the millions on high.

CHORUS.

He hid-eth my soul in the cleft of the rock, That shadows a dry, thirsty land; He hid-eth my life in the depths of His love, And cov-ers me there with His hand, And covers me there with His hand.

Copyright, 1890, by Wm. J. Kirkpatrick.

Come Home To-night. Concluded.

pleading come home to-night, Come home, ... come home, ...
Come home to-night, come home to-night, come home to-night,

O hear His tender pleading, come home, come home to-night.

No. 37. Pass Me Not.

FANNY J. CROSBY.   W. H. DOANE.

1. Pass me not, O gentle Saviour, Hear my humble cry; While on
2. Let me at a throne of mercy Find a sweet relief; Kneeling
3. Trusting only in Thy merit, Would I seek Thy face; Heal my
4. Thou the Spring of all my comfort, More than life to me, Whom have

CHORUS.

others Thou art smiling, Do not pass me by.
there in deep contrition, Help my unbelief.
wounded, broken spirit, Save me by Thy grace.
I on earth beside Thee? Whom in heav'n but Thee?

Saviour, Saviour,

Hear my humble cry, While on others Thou art calling, Do not pass me by.

Copyright, 1870, by W. H. Doane. Used by per.

No. 38. Whiter than Snow.

JAMES NICHOLSON.   WM. G. FISCHER.

1. Lord Jesus, I long to be perfectly whole; I want Thee forever to live in my soul; Break down ev'ry idol, cast out ev'ry foe; Now wash me, and I shall be
2. Lord Jesus, look down from Thy throne in the skies, And help me to make a complete sacrifice; I give up myself, and whatever I know—Now wash me, and I shall be
3. Lord Jesus, for this I most humbly entreat; I wait, blessed Lord, at Thy crucified feet; By faith, for my cleansing, I see Thy blood flow—Now wash me, and I shall be
4. Lord Jesus, Thou seest I patiently wait; Come now, and within me a new heart create; To those who have sought Thee, Thou never said'st No—Now wash me, and I shall be

CHORUS.

whiter than snow, Whiter than snow, yes, whiter than snow; Now wash me, and I shall be whiter than snow.

Used by per. of W. G. Fischer, owner of copyright.

By and By. Concluded.

rest for-ev - er - more, By and by, By and by.
glo - ry we shall rise, By and by, By and by.
oth - er's face we view, By and by, By and by.

By and by, ... By and by.

No. 41. Anywhere With Jesus is Home to Me.

Rev. J. G. BONNELL.   J. F. M. Arr. by J. M. BLACK.

1. If Jesus is my Broth-er, And God my Fa-ther be;
2. Tho' I roam the wide world o - ver, And trav-erse ma-ny a sea,
3. Tho' from other friends di - vid - ed, His pres-ence will not flee;

Then an - y-where with Je - sus Is home, sweet home to me.
Still an - y-where with Je - sus Is home, sweet home to me.
So an - y-where with Je - sus Is home, sweet home to me.

CHORUS.

An - y-where, an - y-where, Wher-ev - er I may be;

An - y-where with Je - sus, Is home, sweet home to me.

Copyright, 1896, by J. M. Black.

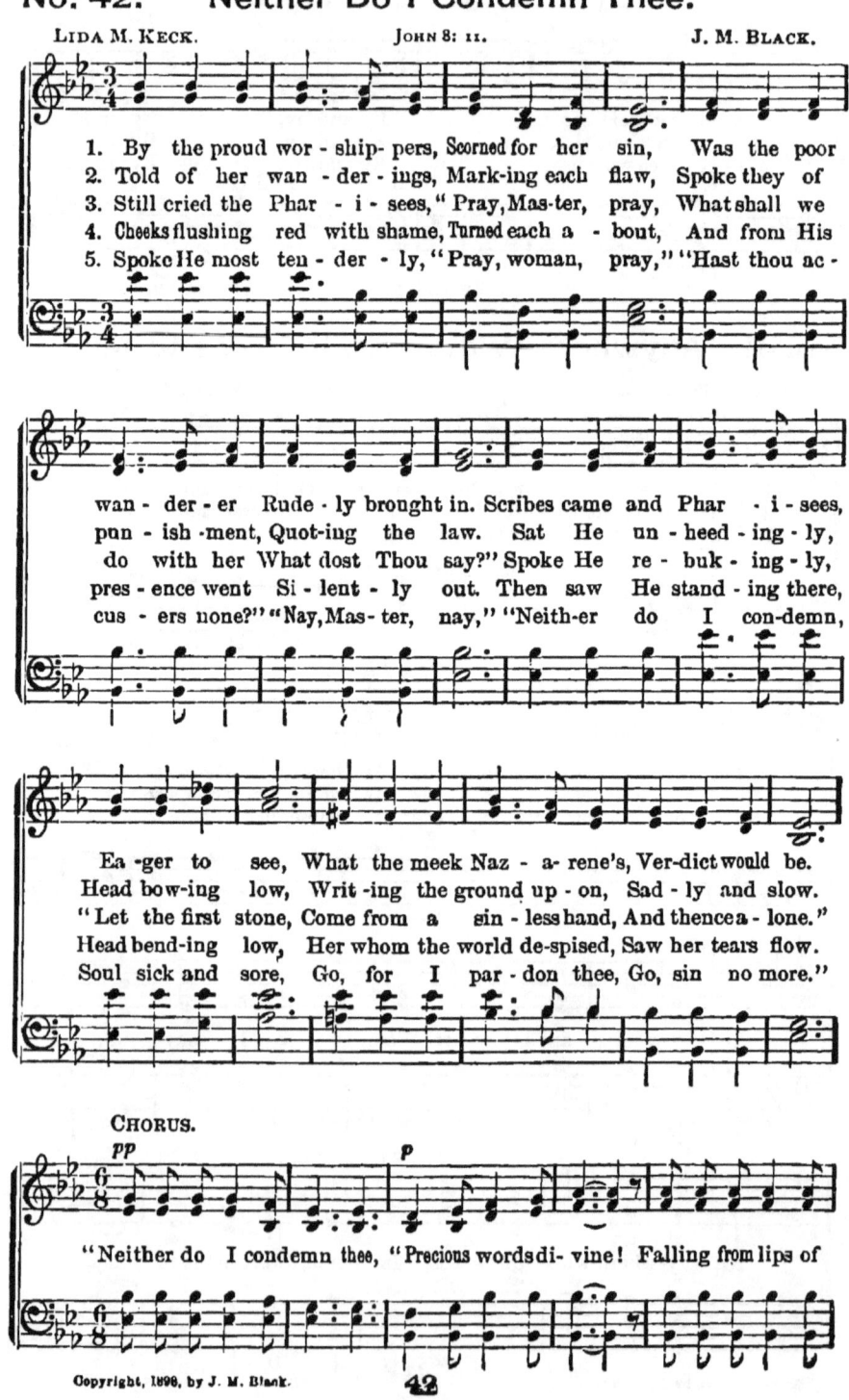

"Neither Do I Condemn Thee." Concluded.

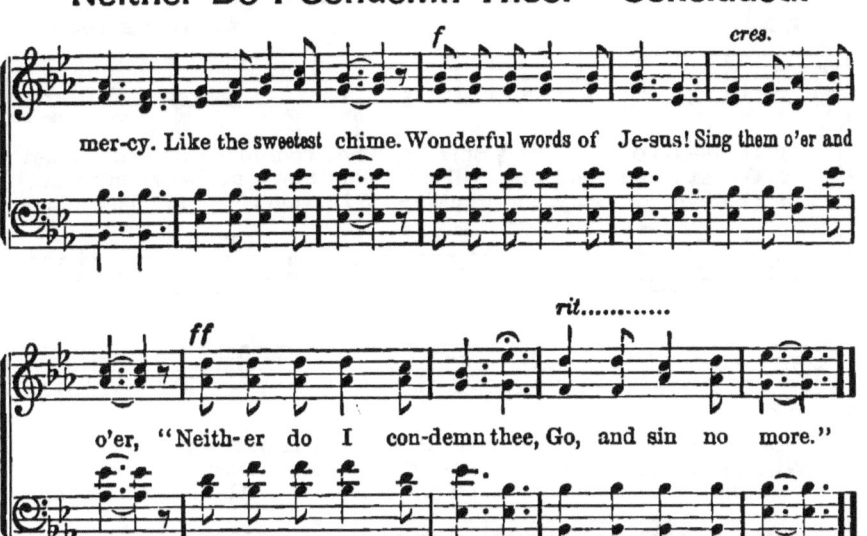

No. 43. Sitting at the Feet of Jesus.

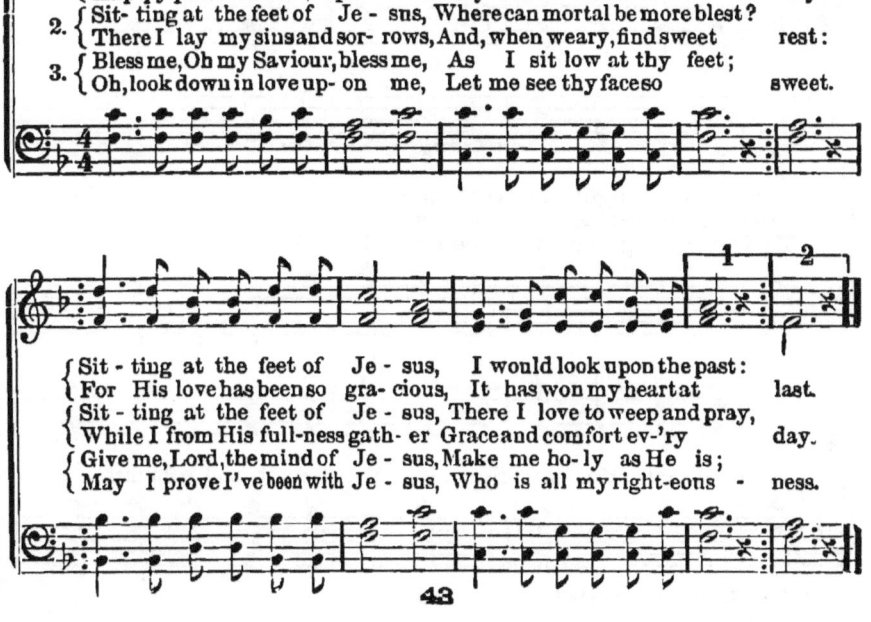

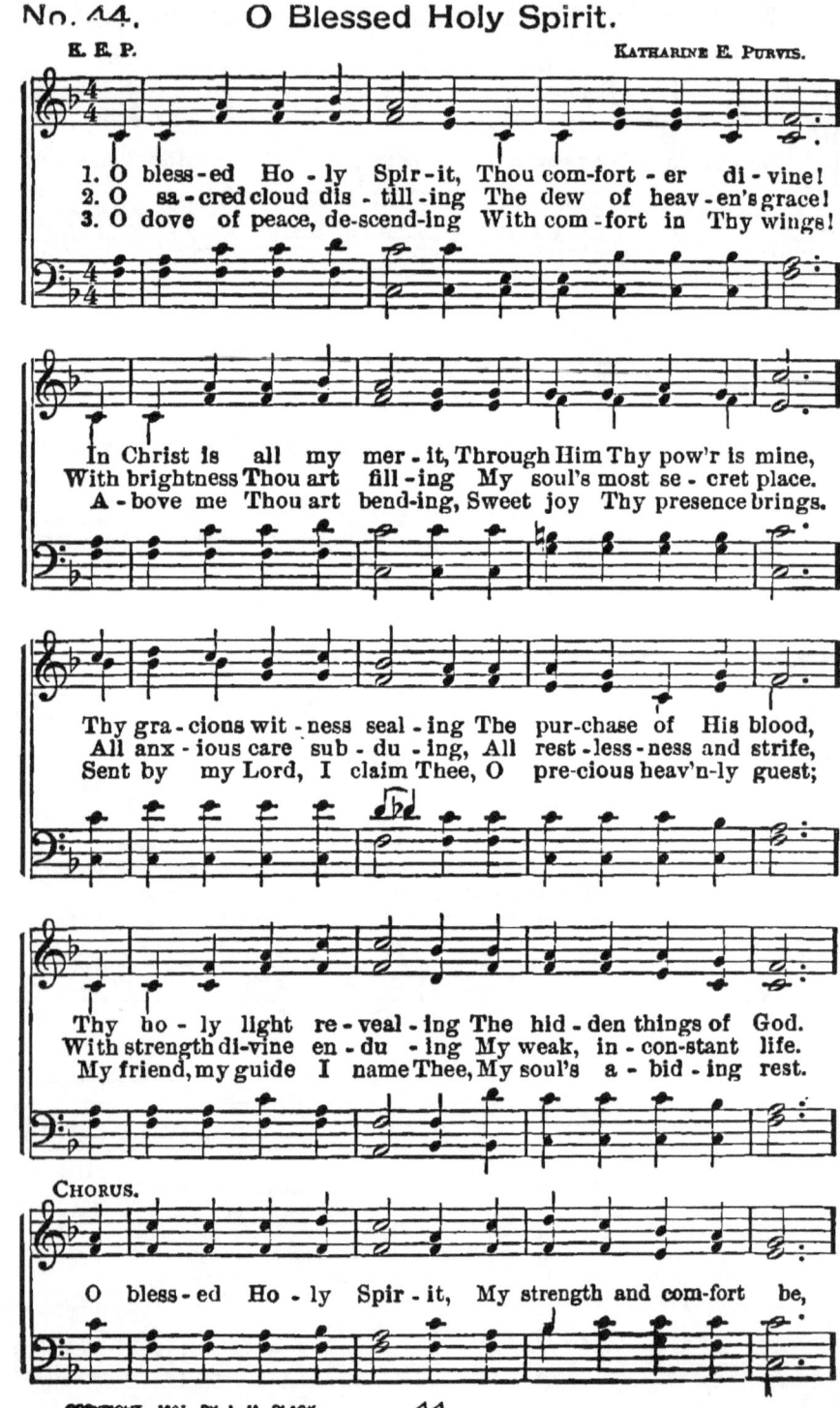

O Blessed Holy Spirit. Concluded.

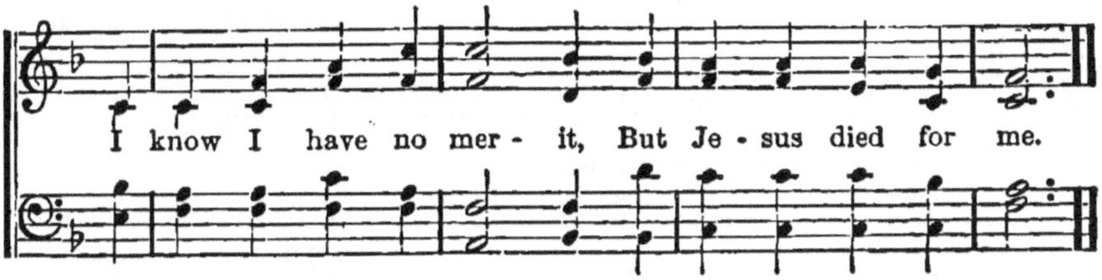

I know I have no mer-it, But Je-sus died for me.

No. 45.   Jesus is Good to Me.

Rev. E. H. Stokes, D.D.   Jno. R. Sweney.

1. I love my Sa-viour, His heart is good, He has loved me o'er and o'er;
2. He calls, I rise, and He maketh me whole,—How fond His tender embrace!
3. I want to love Him with all my heart, Tho' all its powers are small;
4. He's good to me in my sorrow's night, He's good in the tempest's roll;

He sought me wand'ring, I'm saved by His blood, And I love Him more and more.
He cleanses and keeps me and blesses my soul, My day the smile of His face.
I will not keep from Him an-y part, For He is worthy of all.
He bringeth from darkness in-to light,—With joy He fill-eth my soul.

Chorus.

Je-sus is good to me,...... Je-sus is good to me;......
                    to me,   to me;

So good! so good! Je-sus is good to my soul.

Copyright, 1885, by John J. Hood.

No. 48. There'll Be No Dark Valley.

W. O. CUSHING.   IRA D. SANKEY.

1. There'll be no dark val-ley when Je-sus comes, There'll be no dark val-ley when Je-sus comes; There'll be no dark val-ley when
2. There'll be no more sor-row when Je-sus comes, There'll be no more sor-row when Je-sus comes; But a glo-rious morrow when
3. There'll be no more weeping when Je-sus comes, There'll be no more weep-ing when Je-sus comes; But a bless-ed reap-ing when
4. There'll be songs of greeting when Je-sus comes, There'll be songs of greet-ing when Je-sus comes; And a joy-ful meet-ing when

REFRAIN.

Je-sus comes To gather His loved ones home, To gather His loved ones home, safe home, To gath-er His loved ones home; There'll be safe home; no dark val-ley when Je-sus comes To gather His loved ones home.

Copyright, 1896, by The Bigelow & Main Co. Used by per.

No. 50. Heaven's Harvest Home.

"The harvest truly is great, but the laborers are few." Luke 10: 1.

LANTA WILSON SMITH.   J. M. BLACK.

1. There are gold-en sheaves to gath-er ere the an-gel reap-ers come,
2. Cut the tan-gles of temp-ta-tion from the pathway of the weak,
3. When re-lent-less pain and sor-row seem to dim the brightest day,

But the toil-ers in the field are few; While a sin-gle soul is waiting
To the fal-len reach a help-ing hand; Throw the arms of love and sympa-
And the cherished hopes of life decline; Let the dew of love and mercy

to be garnered for the Lord, There is work for human hands to do.
-thy around the err-ing one, Till by faith he learns to firmly stand.
fall from heaven's boundless store Till the world shall glow with light divine.

CHORUS.

Gath - - er, gath - - er,
Gath-er in the golden sheaves, Gather in the golden sheaves, Golden

We must gath - - - er,
sheaves to stand before the throne, Gath-er in the golden sheaves,

COPYRIGHT, 1897, BY J. M. BLACK.

Meet me There. Concluded.

tree of life is bloom-ing, Meet me there, Meet me there;

When the storms of life are o'er, On the

D.S.

No. 55. What a Friend.

H. BONAR.   C. C. CONVERSE. By per.

1. What a friend we have in Je - sus, All our griefs and sins to bear!
What a priv-i-lege to car - ry Ev-'ry-thing to God in prayer!

FINE.

D.S.—All be-cause we do not car - ry Ev-'ry-thing to God in prayer!

Oh, what peace we oft-en for-feit, Oh, what needless pain we bear,

2 Have we trials and temptations?
 Is there trouble anywhere?
We should never be discouraged,
 Take it to the Lord in prayer.
Can we find a friend so faithful,
 Who will all our sorrows share?
Jesus knows our every weakness,
 Take it to the Lord in prayer.

3 Are we weak and heavy-laden,
 Cumbered with a load of care?
Precious Saviour, still our refuge,—
 Take it to the Lord in prayer.
Do thy friends despise, forsake thee?
 Take it to the Lord in prayer.
In His arms He'll take and shield thee,
 Thou wilt find a solace there.

He is Mine, I am His. Concluded.

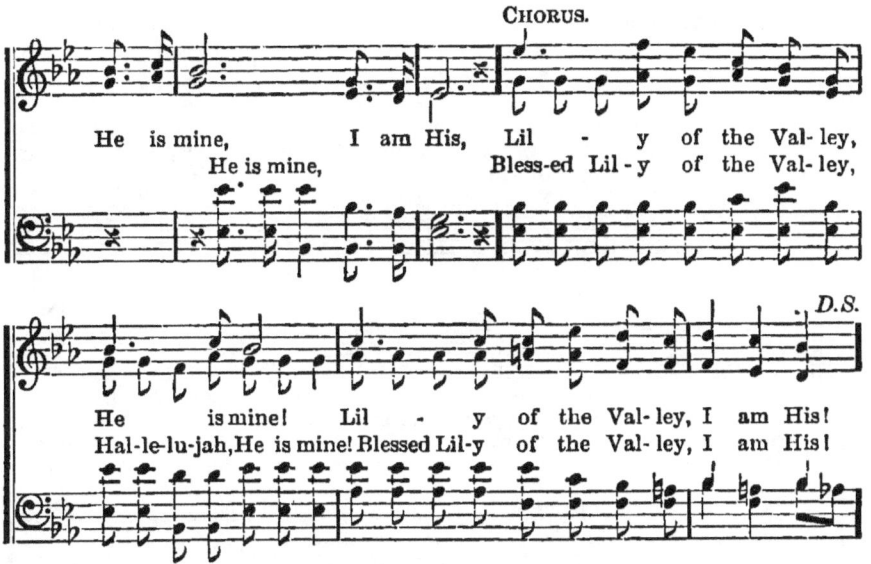

CHORUS.

He is mine, I am His, Lil - y of the Val - ley,
He is mine, Bless-ed Lil - y of the Val - ley,

D.S.

He is mine! Lil - y of the Val - ley, I am His!
Hal-le-lu-jah, He is mine! Blessed Lil-y of the Val - ley, I am His!

No. 59. Nearer, My God to Thee.

SARAH F. ADAMS. LOWELL MASON.

1. Near-er, my God, to Thee, Near-er to Thee; E'en tho' it be a cross
2. Tho, like a wan-der-er, The sun gone down, Darkness be o-ver me,
3. There let the way ap-pear Steps un-to heav'n; All that Thou sendest me,
4. Then with my waking thot's Bright with Thy praise, Out of my ston-y griefs,
5. Or if, on joy-ful wing, Cleaving the sky, Sun, moon, and stars forgot,

D.S.—Near-er, my God, to Thee!

FINE. *D.S.*

That rais-eth me, Still all my song shall be—Near-er, my God, to Thee!
My rest a stone; Yet in my dreams I'd be Near-er, my God, to Thee!
In mer-cy giv'n: An-gels to beckon me Near-er, my God, to Thee!
Beth-el I'll raise; So by my woes to be Near-er, my God, to Thee!
Up-ward I fly, Still all my song shall be, Near-er, my God, to Thee!

Near - er to Thee!

Used by arrangement with Oliver Ditson & Co., owners of copyright.

59

Beautiful Robes. Concluded.

Gar - ments of light,......... Love - ly and bright,......
Garments of light, garments of light, Lovely and bright, lovely and bright,

Walk-ing with Je - sus in white, Beau - ti - ful robes we shall wear.

No. 63. Jesus Will Care for Me.

Rev. E. A. HOFFMAN.   CHAS. H. GABRIEL.

1. Je - sus will care for me, No mat - ter how weak I may be;
2. Je - sus will com - fort me, And make all my sor - row-ing flee;
3. Je - sus will shel - ter me, When I from the dan - ger may flee;

A friend I have found, Whose love will abound, I know He will care for me.
To Him will I cling, My Saviour and King, And Je - sus will comfort me.
The storm-clouds that roll, Cannot harm my soul, For Jesus will shelter me.

Copyright, 1898, by J. M. Blank.

Saviour, Blessed Saviour. Concluded.

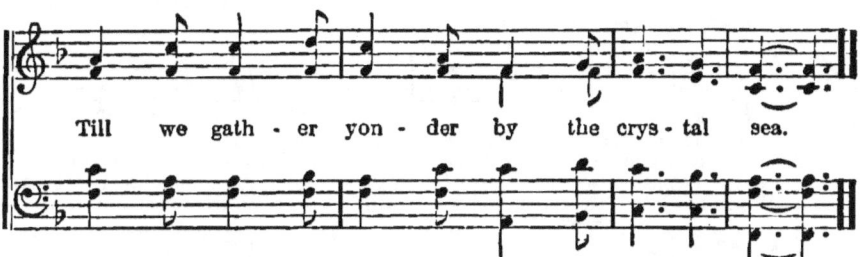

Till we gath-er yon-der by the crys-tal sea.

No. 67.   Abide with Me.

HENRY F. LYTE. WILLIAM HENRY MONK.

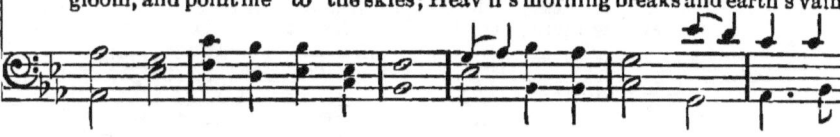

1. A-bide with me! fast falls the ev-en-tide, The dark-ness
2. I need Thy pre-sence ev-'ry pass-ing hour; What but Thy
3. Hold Thou Thy cross be-fore my clos-ing eyes; Shine thro' the

deep-ens; Lord, with me a-bide! When oth-er help-ers fail and
grace can foil the tempter's pow'r? Who like Thy-self my guide and
gloom, and point me to the skies; Heav'n's morning breaks and earth's vain

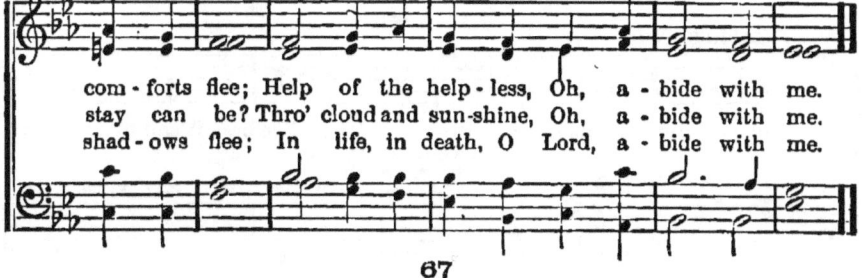

com-forts flee; Help of the help-less, Oh, a-bide with me.
stay can be? Thro' cloud and sun-shine, Oh, a-bide with me.
shad-ows flee; In life, in death, O Lord, a-bide with me.

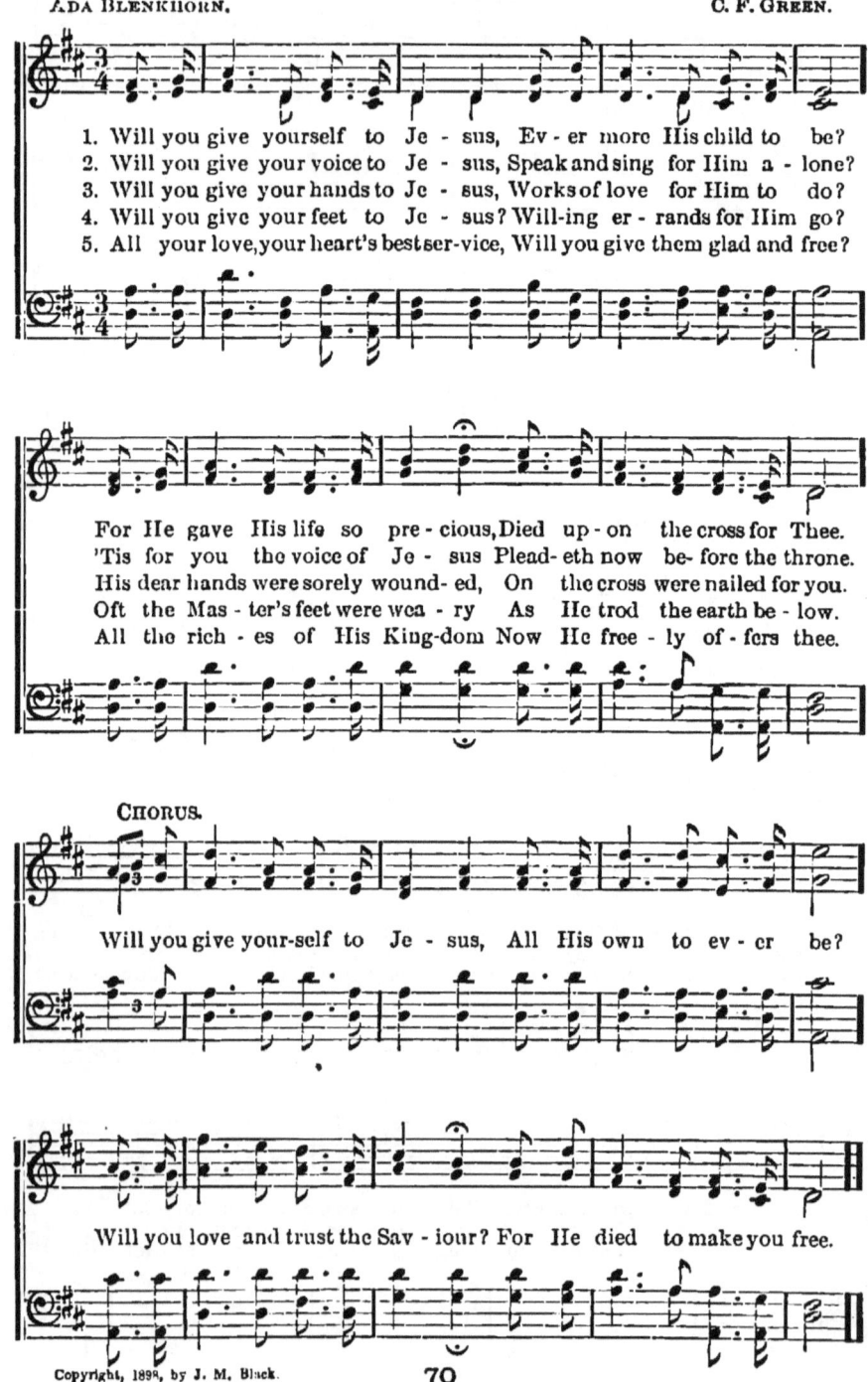

No. 73. Wonderful Peace.

Rev. W. D. Cornell. Alt. Rev. W. G. Cooper.

1. Far a-way in the depths of my spir-it to-night, Rolls a
2. What a treas-ure I have in this won-der-ful peace, Bur-ied
3. I am rest-ing to-night in this won-der-ful peace, Rest-ing
4. And me-thinks when I rise to that Cit-y of peace, Where the
5. Ah! soul are you here with-out com-fort or rest, March-ing

mel-o-dy sweet-er than psalm; In ce-les-tial like strains it un-
deep in the heart of my soul; So se-cure that no pow-er can
sweet-ly in Je-sus' con-trol; For I'm kept from all dan-ger by
Au-thor of peace I shall see, That one strain of the song which the
down the rough pathway of time! Make Je-sus your friend ere the

ceas-ing-ly falls O'er my soul like an in-fi-nite calm.
mine it a-way, While the years of e-ter-ni-ty roll.
night and by day, And His glo-ry is flood-ing my soul.
ran-somed will sing, In that heav-en-ly kingdom shall be:—
shad-ows grow dark; Oh, ac-cept of this peace so sub-lime.

CHORUS.

Peace! peace! Wonder-ful peace, Coming down from the Father a-bove; Sweep
o-ver my spir-it for-ev-er, I pray, In fath-omless billows of love.

Used by permission of D. B. Towner, owner of copyright.

No. 77. Come to Him Now.

KATHARINE E. PURVIS. C. F. GREEN.

1. Je-sus is wait-ing, oh sin-ner, for thee, Call-ing so ten-der-ly, "Come un-to me," Wait-ing His mer-cy and peace to im-part,
2. Come from the path that seems pleasant and wide, Narrow the way if thou walk by His side— Nar-row, yet brighten'd with blessings un-told,
3. Come to the Sav-iour whose grace is so free, Come to Him now while He call-eth for thee, En-ter the fold by the on-ly true door,

CHORUS.

Come then, oh wan-der-er, give Him thy heart.
Lead-ing thee home to the cit-y of gold.
Come, quick-ly come, lest He call thee no more.

Come to Him now, He's waiting for thee, Turn not a-way from His mercy so free, Je-sus is wait-ing, waiting for thee, Call-ing so ten-der-ly, "Come unto Me."

Copyright, 1898, by J. M. Black.

"Whosoever," That means Me. Concluded.

I will love Him, ev - er love Him, "Whoso- ev - er" that means me.

No. 79.   On the Way.

LIZZIE EDWARDS.   JNO. R. SWENEY.

1. Oh, bless the Lord, what joy is mine! What perfect peace thro' grace divine!
2. Oh, bless the Lord, He dwells with me, The voice I hear, the hand I see
3. Oh, bless the Lord for what I know Of heav'nly bliss while here be-low!
4. Oh, bless the Lord 'twill not be long Till I shall join the ho - ly throng,

And now to realms of end-less day, Oh, bless the Lord, I'm on the way.
Re - new my strength from day to day While home to Him I'm on the way.
My trust-ing heart thro' faith can say, To mansions bright I'm on the way.
And shout and sing thro' end-less day, Where ev-'ry tear is wiped a- way.

D.S.—crown to wear in end - less day, Oh, bless the Lord, I'm on the way.

CHORUS.   D.S.

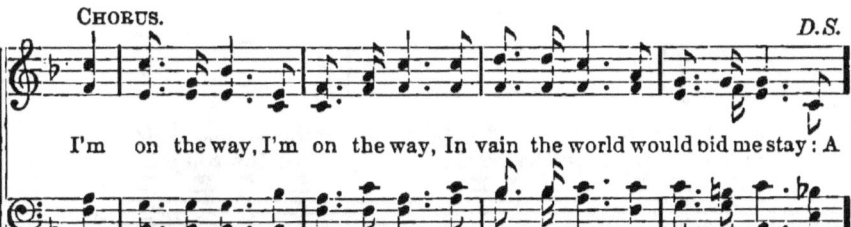

I'm on the way, I'm on the way, In vain the world would bid me stay: A

Copyright, 1890, by Jno. R. Sweney. Used by per.

When the King Shall Come. Concluded.

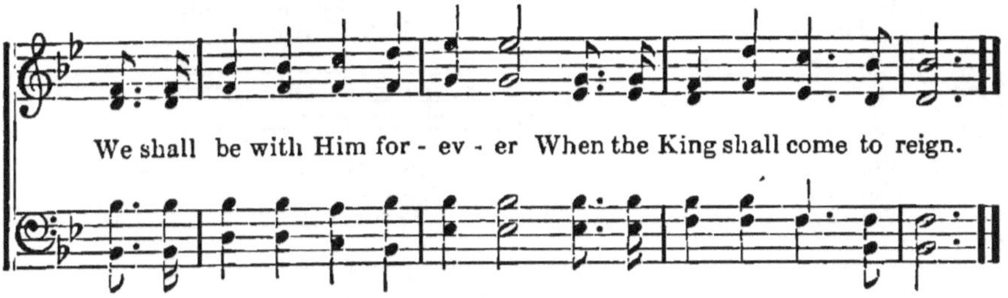

We shall be with Him for-ev-er When the King shall come to reign.

No. 85.   I Need Thee Every Hour.

Mrs. ANNIE E. HAWKES.   Rev. ROBERT LOWRY.

1. I need Thee ev-'ry hour, Most gra-cious Lord; No tender voice like
2. I need Thee ev-'ry hour, Stay Thou near by; Temptations lose their
3. I need Thee ev-'ry hour, In joy or pain; Come quickly and a-
4. I need Thee ev-'ry hour; Teach me Thy will; And Thy rich promis-
5. I need Thee ev-'ry hour, Most Ho-ly One; O make me Thine in-

REFRAIN.

Thine Can peace af-ford.
pow'r When Thou art nigh.
bide, Or life is vain.
es In me ful-fill.
deed, Thou bless-ed Son!

I need Thee, O I need Thee, Ev-'ry hour I need Thee; O bless me now, my Sav-iour, I come to Thee.

Copyright, 1872, by Robert Lowry. Used by per.

85

No. 89. God Be With You.

"Grace be to you and peace from God our Father, and from the Lord Jesus Christ."—2 Cor. 1: 2.

Rev. J. E. RANKIN, D. D.   W. G. TOMER.

1. God be with you till we meet a-gain; By His coun-sels guide, up-hold you, With His sheep se- cure- ly fold you,
2. God be with you till we meet a- gain, 'Neath His wing se- cure- ly hide you; Dai- ly man- na still pro- vide you,
3. God be with you till we meet a- gain, When life's per- ils thick con- found you, Put His arms un- fail- ing round you,
4. God be with you till we meet a- gain, Keep love's ban-ner float-ing o'er you, Smite death's threat'ning wave be- fore you,

CHORUS.

God be with you till we meet a-gain. Till we meet,......... Till we meet, Till we meet, till we meet, Till we meet at Je- sus' feet; Till we meet a-gain, till we meet; Till we meet,........ till we meet God be with you till we meet a-gain. Till we meet, till we meet a-gain,

Copyright by J. E. Rankin, D. D, used by per.

No. 90. Wilt thou be Made Whole?

W. J. K.
Wm. J. Kirkpatrick.

1. Hear the footsteps of Jesus, He is now passing by, Bearing balm for the wounded, Healing all who apply; As He spake to the suff'rer Who lay at the pool, He is saying this moment, "Wilt thou be made whole?"
2. 'Tis the voice of that Saviour, Whose merciful call Freely offers salvation, To one and to all; He is now beck'ning to Him Each sin tainted soul, And lovingly asking, "Wilt thou be made whole?"
3. Are you halting and struggling, O'erpowered by your sin, While the waters are troubled Can you not enter in? Lo, the Saviour stands waiting To strengthen your soul, He is earnestly pleading, "Wilt thou be made whole?"
4. Blessed Saviour, assist us To rest on Thy word; Let the soul-healing power On us now be out-poured: Wash away ev'ry sin-spot, Take perfect control, Say to each trusting spirit, "Thy faith makes thee whole?"

REFRAIN.

Wilt thou be made whole? Wilt thou be made whole? O come, weary suff'rer, O come, sin-sick soul; See, the life-stream is flowing, See the

Used by permission

Wilt thou be Made Whole? Concluded.

cleansing waves roll, Step in-to the cur-rent and thou shalt be whole.

No. 91. Jesus the Light of the World.

G. D. E. arr.
GEO. D. ELDERKIN, arr.

1. Hark! the Her-ald an-gels sing, Je-sus, the Light of the world;
2. Joy-ful, all ye na-tions, rise, Je-sus, the Light of the world;
3. Christ by high-est heav'n a-dored, Je-sus, the Light of the world;
4. Hail the heav'n-born Prince of peace, Je-sus, the Light of the world;

Glo-ry to the new-born King, Jesus, the Light of the world.
Join the tri-umphs of the skies, Jesus, the Light of the world.
Christ, the ev-er-last-ing Lord, Jesus, the Light of the world.
Hail the sun of right-eous-ness, Jesus, the Light of the world.

CHORUS.

We'll walk in the light, beautiful light, Come where the dewdrops of mercy are bright,

Shine all around us by day and by night, Je-sus the light of the world.

Copyright, 1890, by Geo. D. Elderkin, used by per.

Sunlight all the Way. Concluded.

with my Sav-iour near, There is bright and blessed sunlight all the way.

No. 93. The Call for Reapers.

J. O. THOMPSON. J. B. O. CLEMM.

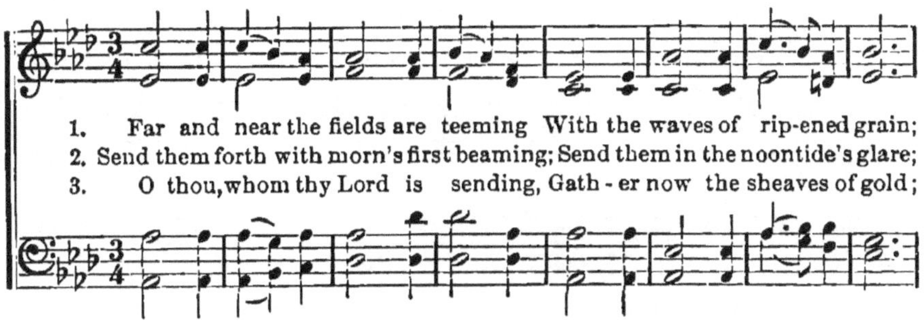

1. Far and near the fields are teeming With the waves of rip-ened grain;
2. Send them forth with morn's first beaming; Send them in the noontide's glare;
3. O thou, whom thy Lord is sending, Gath-er now the sheaves of gold;

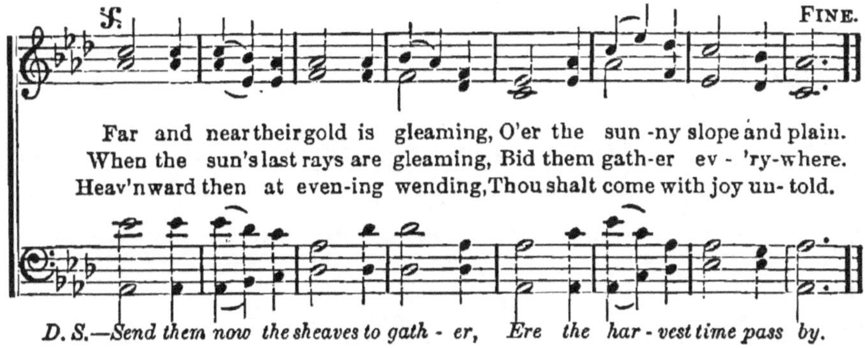

Far and near their gold is gleaming, O'er the sun-ny slope and plain.
When the sun's last rays are gleaming, Bid them gath-er ev-'ry-where.
Heav'nward then at even-ing wending, Thou shalt come with joy un-told.

D. S.—Send them now the sheaves to gath-er, Ere the har-vest time pass by.

CHORUS.

Lord of har-vest, send forth reapers! Hear us Lord, to Thee we cry;

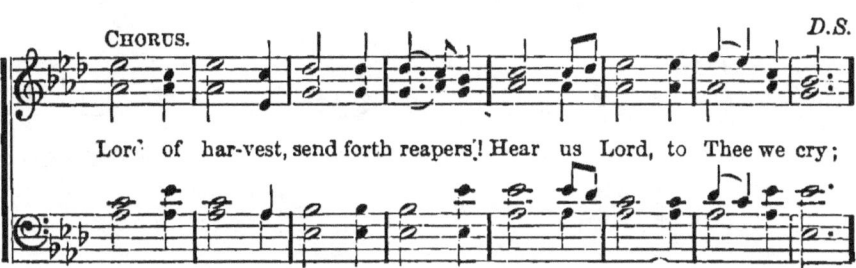

By per. Eaton & Mains, agents, owners of copyright.

It was Spoken, etc.—Concluded.

To the fold of grace may gather Souls of which we lit-tle dream.

No. 95. Glory to His Name.

Rev. E. A. HOFFMAN. Rev. J. H. STOCKTON.

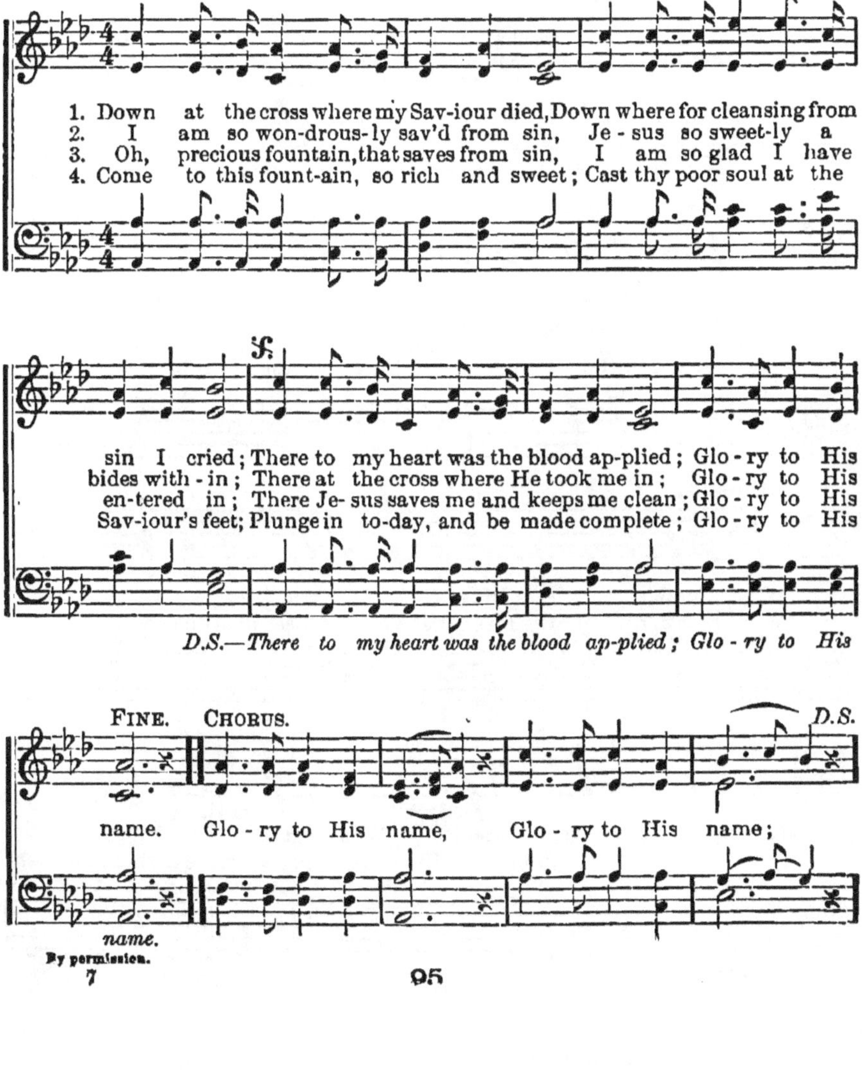

1. Down at the cross where my Sav-iour died, Down where for cleansing from
2. I am so won-drous-ly sav'd from sin, Je-sus so sweet-ly a
3. Oh, precious fountain, that saves from sin, I am so glad I have
4. Come to this fount-ain, so rich and sweet; Cast thy poor soul at the

sin I cried; There to my heart was the blood ap-plied; Glo-ry to His
bides with-in; There at the cross where He took me in; Glo-ry to His
en-tered in; There Je-sus saves me and keeps me clean; Glo-ry to His
Sav-iour's feet; Plunge in to-day, and be made complete; Glo-ry to His

D.S.—There to my heart was the blood ap-plied; Glo-ry to His

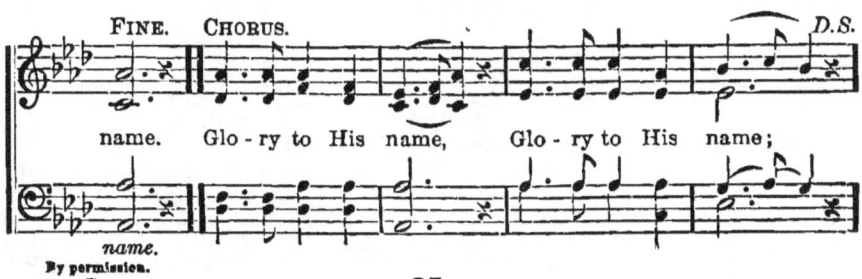

name. Glo-ry to His name, Glo-ry to His name;

name.
By permission.

No. 96. What a Gathering That Will Be.

J. H. K.
J. H. KURZENKNABE.

1. At the sounding of the trumpet, when the saints are gathered home, We will greet each oth-er by the crystal sea, With the friends and all the lov'd ones there a-wait-ing us to come, What a gath'ring of the faith-ful that will be!
2. When the an-gel of the Lord proclaims that time shall be no more, We shall gather, and the saved and ransomed see, Then to meet a-gain togeth-er on the bright ce-les-tial shore, What a gath'ring of the faith-ful that will be!
3. At the great and fi-nal judgment, when the hidden comes to light, When the Lord in all His glo-ry we shall see; At the bidding of our Saviour, "Come, ye bless-ed to my right," What a gath'ring of the faith-ful that will be!
4. When the golden harps are soun-ding, and the angel bands proclaim, In tri-umphant strains the glorious jubilee; Then to meet and join to sing the song of Mo-ses and the Lamb, What a gath'ring of the faith-ful that will be!

CHORUS.

What a gath - - 'ring, gath - - 'ring, At the sounding of the glorious ju-bi-lee! What a gath - 'ring,
What a gath'ring of the loved ones when we meet with one another, ju-bi-lee! What a gath'ring when the friends and all the

From "Song Treasury" by per.

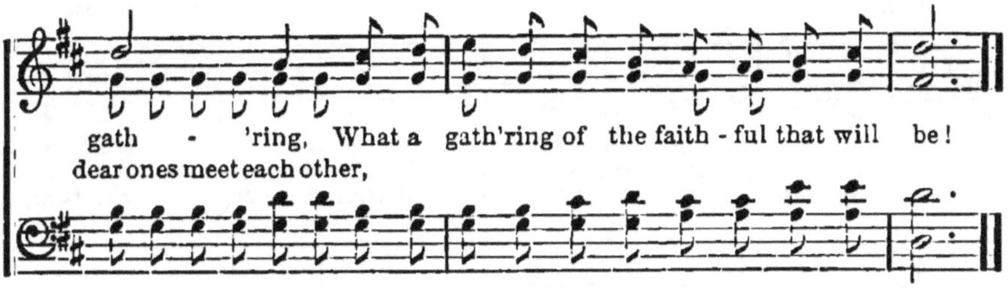

What a Gathering That Will be. Concluded.

gath - 'ring, What a gath'ring of the faith - ful that will be!
dear ones meet each other,

No. 97.   Step Out on the Promise.

MAGGIE POTTER   Arr. by E. F. M.   E. F. MILLER.

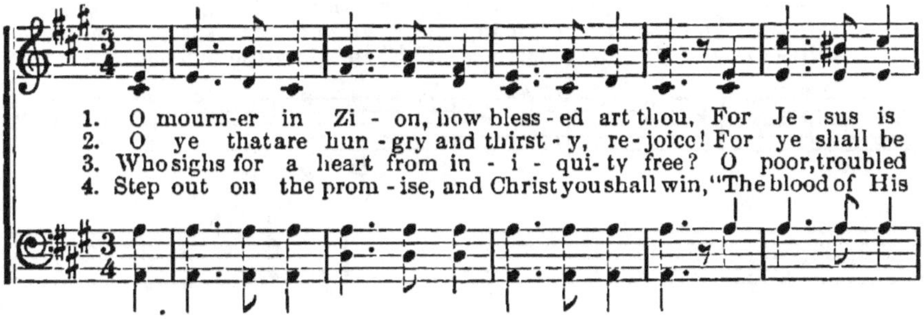

1. O mourn-er in Zi - on, how bless - ed art thou, For Je - sus is
2. O ye that are hun - gry and thirst - y, re - joice! For ye shall be
3. Who sighs for a heart from in - i - qui - ty free? O poor, troubled
4. Step out on the prom - ise, and Christ you shall win, "The blood of His

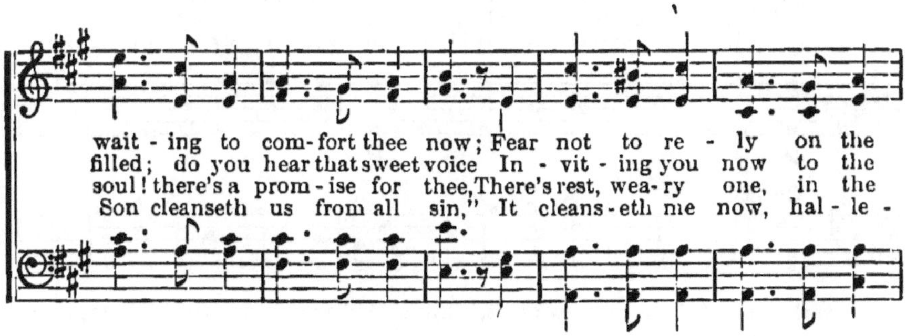

wait - ing to com - fort thee now; Fear not to re - ly on the
filled; do you hear that sweet voice In - vit - ing you now to the
soul! there's a prom - ise for thee, There's rest, wea - ry one, in the
Son cleanseth us from all sin," It cleans - eth me now, hal - le -

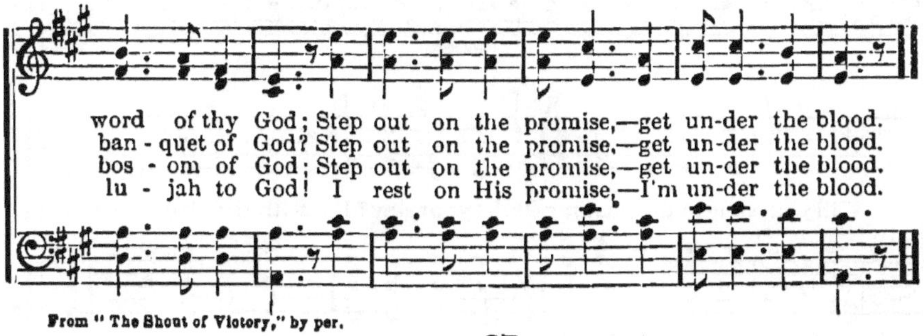

word of thy God; Step out on the promise,—get un-der the blood.
ban - quet of God? Step out on the promise,—get un-der the blood.
bos - om of God; Step out on the promise,—get un-der the blood.
lu - jah to God! I rest on His promise,—I'm un-der the blood.

From "The Shout of Victory," by per.

No. 99. Scattering Precious Seed.

W. A. OGDEN.
GEO. C. HUGG.

1. Scat-ter-ing pre-cious seed by the way-side, Scat-ter-ing pre-cious seed by the hill-side; Scat-ter-ing pre-cious seed o'er the field wide, Scat-ter-ing pre-cious seed by the way.
2. Scat-ter-ing pre-cious seed for the grow-ing, Scat-ter-ing pre-cious seed free-ly sow-ing; Scat-ter-ing pre-cious seed trust-ing, know-ing, Sure-ly the Lord will send it the rain.
3. Scat-ter-ing pre-cious seed, doubt-ing nev-er, Scat-ter-ing pre-cious seed, trust-ing ev-er; Sow-ing the word with pray'r and en-deav-or, Trust-ing the Lord for growth and for yield.

CHORUS.

Sow - - ing in the morn - - ing, Sow - - - ing at the noon - - tide; Sow-ing the pre-cious seed by the way.........
Sow - - ing in the eve - - ning, Sowing the precious seed; by the way.
Sowing the precious seed, Sowing the precious seed, Sowing the seed at noontide,

By per. of Geo. C. Hugg, owner of copyright.

No. 102. Jesus is Passing This Way.

Rev. E. A. Hoffman.   J. H. Tenney.

1. Is there a sin - ner a - wait - ing Mer-cy and par-don to- day?
2. Brother, the Mas- ter is wait - ing, Waiting to free-ly for-give;
3. Yes, He is com- ing to bless you While in con-tri-tion you bow;

Wel-come the news that we bring Him: "Je-sus is passing this way!"
Why not this mo-ment ac- cept Him, Trust in His grace and live?
Com-ing from sin to re - deem you, Read-y to save you now;

Com-ing in love and in mer - cy, Par-don and peace to be - stow,
He is so ten- der and pre-cious, He is so near you to - day;
Can you re-fuse the sal - va - tion Je- sus is of - fer- ing here?

Com-ing to save the poor sin - ner From His heart-anguish and woe.
O - pen your heart to re - ceive Him, While He is pass-ing this way.
O - pen your heart to ad- mit Him, While He is com-ing so near.

CHORUS.

Je-sus is passing this way . . . To - day, . . . to - day, . . .
Je-sus is passing this way, To-day, is pass-ing to-day!

Copyright, 1887, by E. A. Hoffman. Used by permission.

Jesus is Passing This Way. Concluded.

While He is near, O be-lieve Him, Open your heart to receive Him, For

Je-sus is pass-ing this way, . . Is passing this way to-day.
this way,

No. 103.   **The Way of the Cross.**

Arr.

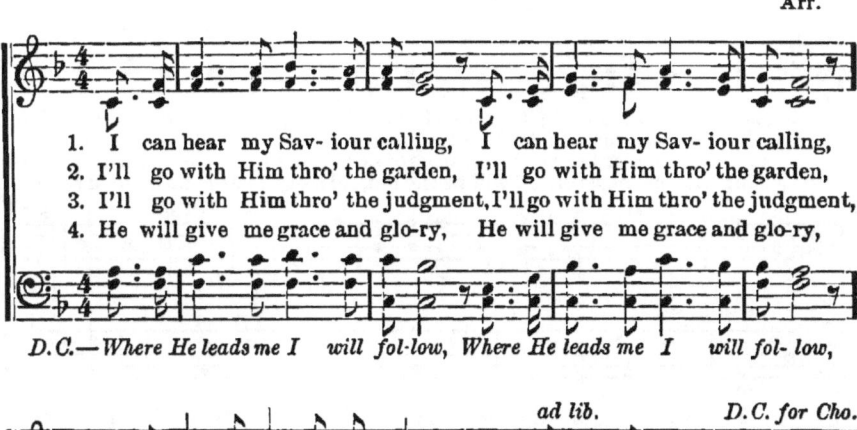

1. I can hear my Sav-iour calling, I can hear my Sav-iour calling,
2. I'll go with Him thro' the garden, I'll go with Him thro' the garden,
3. I'll go with Him thro' the judgment, I'll go with Him thro' the judgment,
4. He will give me grace and glo-ry, He will give me grace and glo-ry,

D.C.—Where He leads me I will fol-low, Where He leads me I will fol-low,

ad lib.   D.C. for Cho.

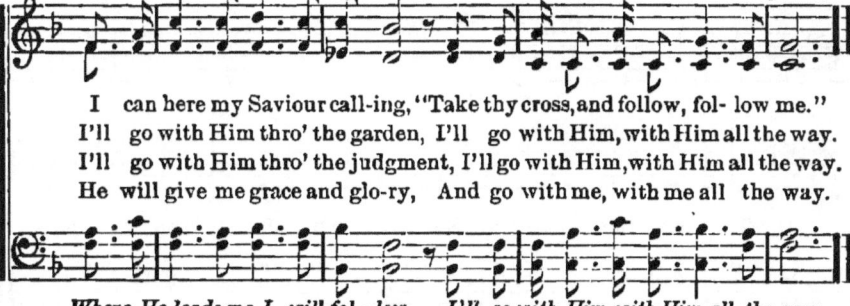

I can here my Saviour call-ing, "Take thy cross, and follow, fol-low me."
I'll go with Him thro' the garden, I'll go with Him, with Him all the way.
I'll go with Him thro' the judgment, I'll go with Him, with Him all the way.
He will give me grace and glo-ry, And go with me, with me all the way.

Where He leads me I will fol-low, I'll go with Him, with Him all the way.

I'll Go where You want Me to Go. Concluded.

I'll say what you want me to say, dear Lord, I'll be what you want me to be.

No. 107.   **No, Not One.**

Rev. JOHNSON OATMAN.   GEO. C. HUGG.
Slow, and with great feeling.

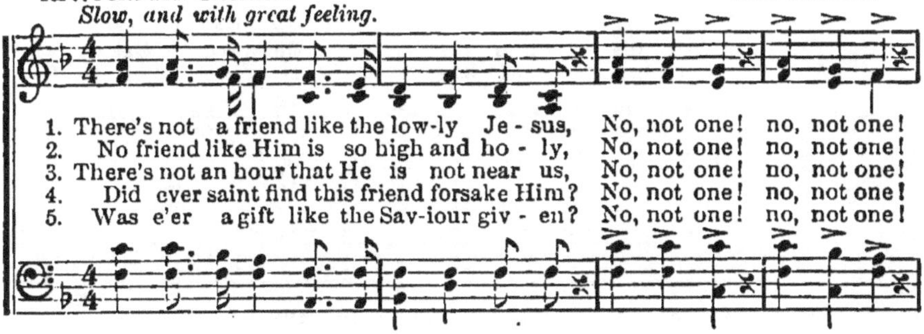

1. There's not a friend like the low-ly Je-sus, No, not one! no, not one!
2. No friend like Him is so high and ho-ly, No, not one! no, not one!
3. There's not an hour that He is not near us, No, not one! no, not one!
4. Did ever saint find this friend forsake Him? No, not one! no, not one!
5. Was e'er a gift like the Sav-iour giv-en? No, not one! no, not one!

None else could heal all our soul's dis-eas-es, No, not one! no, not one!
And yet no friend is so meek and low-ly, No, not one! no, not one!
No night so dark but His love can cheer us, No, not one! no, not one!
Or sinner find that He would not take Him? No, not one! no, not one!
Will He re-fuse us a home in heav-en? No, not one! no, not one!

D.S.—There's not a friend like the low-ly Je-sus, No, not one! no, not one!

CHORUS.

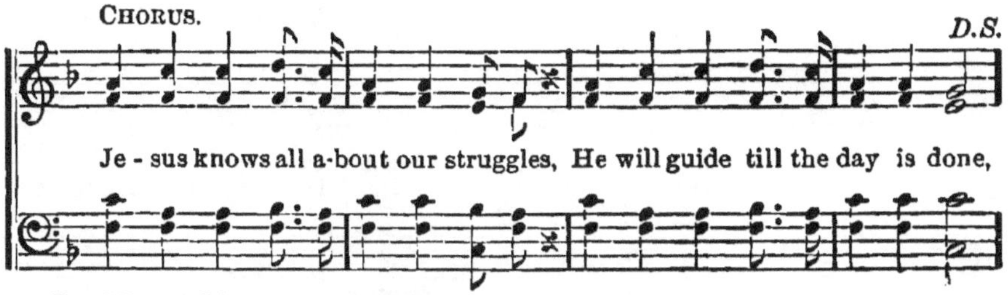

Je-sus knows all a-bout our struggles, He will guide till the day is done,

From "Heaven's Echo," by per. of Geo. C. Hugg.

107

No. 108. Just the Same To-Day.

Mrs. S. Z. Kaufman.   W. A. Ogden.

1. Have you ev-er heard the sto-ry Of the Babe of Beth-le-hem,
2. Have you ev-er heard the sto-ry How He walked upon the sea,
3. Have you ev-er heard of Je-sus, Pray-ing in Geth-sem-a-ne,

Who was wor-shipped by the an-gels, And the wise and ho-ly men?
To His dear dis-ci-ples toss-ing, On the waves of Gal-i-lee?
And the ev-er-thrill-ing sto-ry How He died up-on the tree,

How He taught the learn-ed doc-tors In the tem-ple far a-way?
How the waves, in an-gry mo-tion, Quick-ly at His will a-bey?
Cru-el thorns His fore-head pierc-ing, As His spir-it passed a-way?

Oh, I'm glad, so glad to tell you, He is just the same to-day!
Oh, I'm glad, so glad to tell you, He is just the same to-day!
This He did for you, my broth-er, And He's just the same to-day!

CHORUS.

He is just............ the same to-day,
Just the same to-day, He is just the same to-day,

By permission.

No. 111.   **How Firm a Foundation.**

G. KEITH.   Portuguese Hymn. 11s.   M. PORTOGALLO.

1. How firm a foun-da-tion, ye saints of the Lord, Is laid for your faith in His ex-cellent word! What more can He say, than to you He hath said,—To you, who for ref-uge to Je-sus have fled? To you, who for ref-uge to Je-sus have fled?
2. "Fear not, I am with thee, oh be not dismayed, For I am thy God, I will still give thee aid; I'll strengthen thee, help thee, and cause thee to stand, Upheld by My gracious, om-nip-o-tent hand, Up-held by My gra-cious om-nip-o-tent hand.
3. "When thro' the deep waters I call thee to go, The riv-ers of sorrow shall not o-ver-flow; For I will be with thee thy troub-le to bless, And sanc-ti-fy to thee thy deep-est dis-tress, And sanc-ti-fy to thee thy deepest dis-tress.
4. "The soul that on Je-sus hath leaned for re-pose, I will not—I will not de-sert to His foes; That soul—tho' all hell should endeavor to shake, I'll never—no, nev-er—no, nev-er for-sake!" I'll nev-er—no, nev-er—no, nev-er for-sake!"

No. 112.   **Just as I Am.**

CHARLOTTE ELLIOTT.   WM. B. BRADBURY.

1. Just as I am, with-out one plea, But that Thy blood was shed for me,
2. Just as I am, and wait-ing not To rid my soul of one dark blot,
3. Just as I am, tho' tossed a-bout, With many a con-flict, many a doubt,
4. Just as I am, poor, wretched, blind, Sight, rich-es, heal-ing of the mind,
5. Just as I am, Thou wilt re-ceive, Wilt wel-come, pardon, cleanse, relieve;

No. 113. There is a Fountain.

W. COWPER. LOWELL MASON.

1. There is a fount-ain filled with blood, Drawn from Im-man-uel's veins;
2. The dy-ing thief re-joiced to see That fount-ain in his day;
3. Dear dy-ing Lamb, Thy pre-cious blood Shall nev-er lose its power,
4. E'er since, by faith, I saw the stream Thy flow-ing wounds sup-ply,
5. Then in a no-bler, sweet-er song, I'll sing Thy power to save,

And sin-ners plunged be-neath that flood, Lose all their guilt-y stains.
And there may I, though vile as he, Wash all my sins a-way.
Till all the ran-somed church of God Be saved to sin no more,
Re-deem-ing love has been my theme, And shall be, till I die,
When this poor lisp-ing, stammering tongue, Lies si-lent in the grave,

Lose all their guilt-y stains,...... Lose all their guilt-y stains.
Wash all my sins a-way,.......... Wash all my sins a-way.
Be saved to sin no more,........ Be saved to sin no more.
And shall be, till I die,........... And shall be, till I die.
Lies si-lent in the grave,...... Lies si-lent in the grave.

No. 114. My Faith Looks Up to Thee.

RAY PALMER. L. MASON.

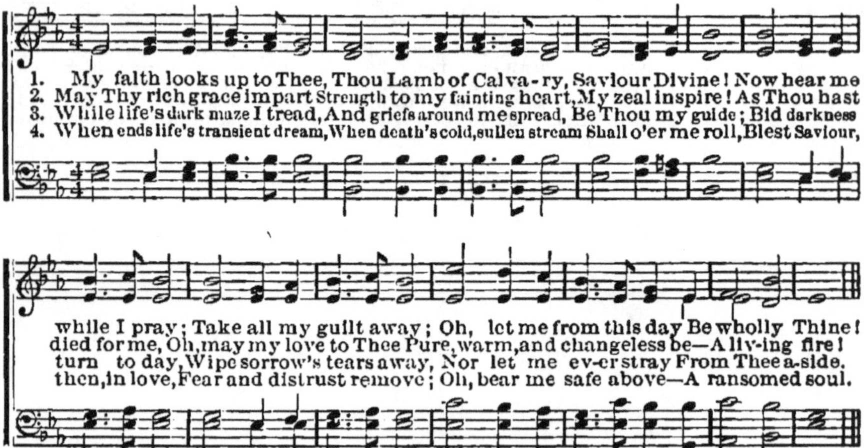

1. My faith looks up to Thee, Thou Lamb of Calva-ry, Saviour Divine! Now hear me
2. May Thy rich grace impart Strength to my fainting heart, My zeal inspire! As Thou hast
3. While life's dark maze I tread, And griefs around me spread, Be Thou my guide; Bid darkness
4. When ends life's transient dream, When death's cold, sullen stream Shall o'er me roll, Blest Saviour,

while I pray; Take all my guilt away; Oh, let me from this day Be wholly Thine!
died for me, Oh, may my love to Thee Pure, warm, and changeless be—A liv-ing fire!
turn to day, Wipe sorrow's tears away, Nor let me ev-er stray From Thee a-side.
then, in love, Fear and distrust remove; Oh, bear me safe above—A ransomed soul.

No. 115. Take my Life and Let it Be.

FRANCES R. HAVERGAL. C. H. A. MALAN.

No. 116. Come, my Soul.

1 Come, my soul, thy suit prepare,
Jesus loves to answer prayer;
He Himself invites thee near,
Bids thee ask Him, waits to hear.

2 Lord, I come to Thee for rest;
Take possession of my breast;
There Thy blood-bought right maintain,
And without a rival reign.

3 While I am a pilgrim here,
Let Thy love my spirit cheer;
As my Guide, my Guard, my Friend,
Lead me to my journey's end.

4 Show me what I have to do;
Every hour my strength renew;
Let me live a life of faith,
Let me die Thy people's death.
John Newton.

No. 117. They who Seek.

1 They who seek the throne of grace,
Find that throne in every place;
If we live a life of prayer,
God is present everywhere.

2 In our sickness or our health,
In our want or in our wealth,
If we look to God in prayer,
God is present everywhere.

3 When our earthly comforts fail,
When the foes of life prevail,
'Tis the time for earnest prayer;
God is present everywhere.

4 Then my soul, in every strait
To thy Father come and wait;
He will answer every prayer;
God is present everywhere.
Oliver Holden, alt.

No. 118. Gracious Spirit.

1 Gracious Spirit, Love Divine,
Let Thy light within me shine!
All my guilty fears remove;
Fill me with Thy heavenly love.

2 Speak Thy pardoning grace to me;
Set the burdened sinner free;
Lead me to the Lamb of God:
Wash me in His precious blood.

3 Life and peace to me impart;
Seal salvation on my heart;
Breathe Thyself into my breast,
Earnest of immortal rest.

4 Let me never from Thee stray;
Keep me in the narrow way;
Fill my soul with joy divine;
Keep me, Lord, forever Thine.
John Stocker.

No. 119. Come, Sound His Praise.

ISAAC WATTS.   ISAAC SMITH.

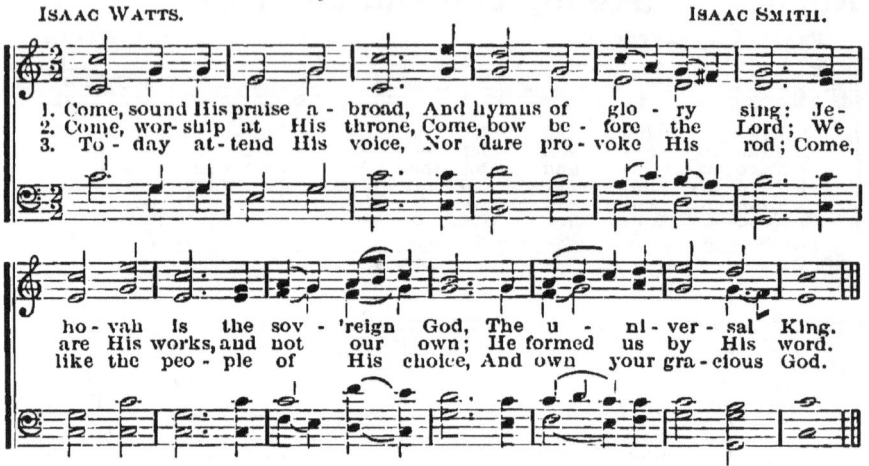

1. Come, sound His praise a-broad, And hymns of glory sing: Jehovah is the sov-'reign God, The u-ni-ver-sal King.
2. Come, wor-ship at His throne, Come, bow be-fore the Lord; Great are His works, and not our own; He formed us by His word.
3. To-day at-tend His voice, Nor dare pro-voke His rod; Come, like the peo-ple of His choice, And own your gra-cious God.

No. 120. My Spirit, On Thy Care.

1 My spirit, on Thy care,
  Blest Saviour, I recline;
Thou wilt not leave me to despair,
  For Thou art Love divine.

2 In Thee I place my trust,
  On Thee I calmly rest;
I know Thee good, I know Thee just,
  And count Thy choice the best.

3 Whate'er events betide,
  Thy will they all perform;
Safe in Thy breast my head I hide,
  Nor fear the coming storm.

4 Let good or ill befall,
  It must be good for me;
Secure of having Thee in all,
  Of having all in Thee.
            Henry F. Lyte.

No. 121. Awake, and Sing.

1 Awake, and sing the song
  Of Moses and the Lamb;
Wake, every heart and every tongue,
  To praise the Saviour's name.

2 Sing of His dying love;
  Sing of His rising power;
Sing how He intercedes above
  For those whose sins He bore.

3 Sing on your heavenly way,
  Ye ransomed sinners, sing;
Sing on, rejoicing every day
  In Christ, th' eternal King.

4 Soon shall we hear him say,
  "Ye blessed children, come!"
Soon will He call us hence away,
  To our eternal home.
            William Hammond.

Pleyel's Hymn.

IGNACE PLEYEL.

No. 122. Songs of Praise.

1 Songs of praise the angels sang,
Heaven with hallelujahs rang,
When Jehovah's work begun,
When He spake and it was done.

2 Songs of praise awoke the morn,
When the Prince of Peace was born:
Songs of praise arose, when He
Captive led captivity.

3 Saints below, with heart and voice,
Still in songs of praise rejoice;
Learning here, by faith and love,
Songs of praise to sing above.

4 Borne upon their latest breath,
Songs of praise shall conquer death;
Then amid eternal joy,
Songs of praise their powers employ.
            James Montgomery.

No. 123. Hasten, Sinner.

1 Hasten, sinner, to be wise!
  Stay not for the morrow's sun:
Wisdom if you still despise,
  Harder is it to be won.

2 Hasten, mercy to implore!
  Stay not for the morrow's sun,
Lest thy season should be o'er
  Ere this evening's stage be run.

3 Hasten, sinner, to return!
  Stay not for the morrow's sun,
Lest thy lamp should fail to burn
  Ere salvation's work is done.

4 Hasten, sinner, to be blest!
  Stay not for the morrow's sun,
Lest perdition thee arrest
  Ere the morrow is begun.
            Thomas Scott.

No. 124. Joy to the World.

I. WATTS.   HANDEL.

1. Joy to the world! the Lord is come; Let earth re-ceive her King; Let ev-'ry heart pre-pare him room, And heav'n and na-ture sing, And heav'n and na-ture sing, And heav'n, and heav'n and na-ture sing.
2. Joy to the world! the Sav-iour reigns; Let men their songs employ; While fields and flocks, rocks, hills and plains, Re-peat the sound-ing joy, Re-peat the sound-ing joy, Re-peat, re-peat the sound-ing joy.
3. No more let sin and sor-row grow, Nor thorns in-fest the ground; He comes to make His bless-ings flow Far as the curse is found, Far as the curse is found, Far as, far as the curse is found.
4. He rules the world with truth and grace, And makes the na-tions prove The glo-ries of His right-cous-ness, And won-ders of His love, And won-ders of His love, And won, and won-ders of His love.

No. 125. Work, for the Night is Coming.

ANNIE L. WALKER.   LOWELL MASON.

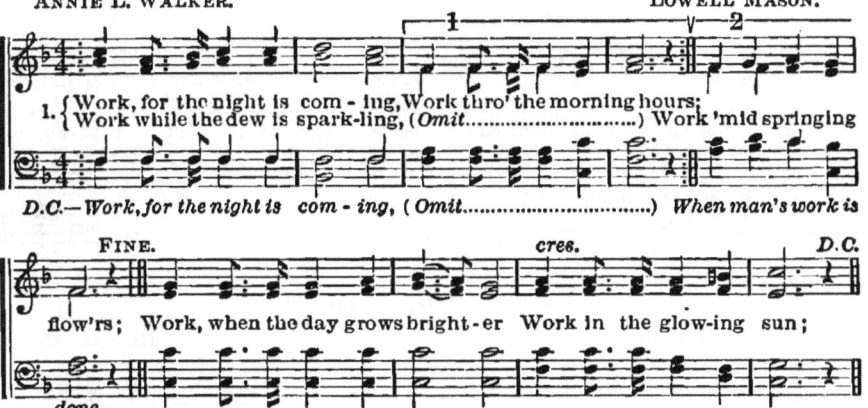

1. { Work, for the night is com-ing, Work thro' the morning hours;
   Work while the dew is spark-ling, (Omit................) Work 'mid springing flow'rs; Work, when the day grows bright-er Work in the glow-ing sun;

D.C.—Work, for the night is com-ing, (Omit................) When man's work is done.

2 Work, for the night is coming,
   Work through the sunny noon;
   Fill brightest hours with labor,
   Rest comes sure and soon;
   Give every flying minute,
   Something to keep in store;
   Work, for the night is coming,
   When man works no more.

3 Work, for the night is coming,
   Under the sunset skies;
   While their bright tints are glowing,
   Work, for daylight flies;
   Work till the last beam fadeth,
   Fadeth to shine no more;
   Work while the night is darkening,
   When man's work is o'er.

Used by arr. with O. Ditson & Co., owners of copyright.

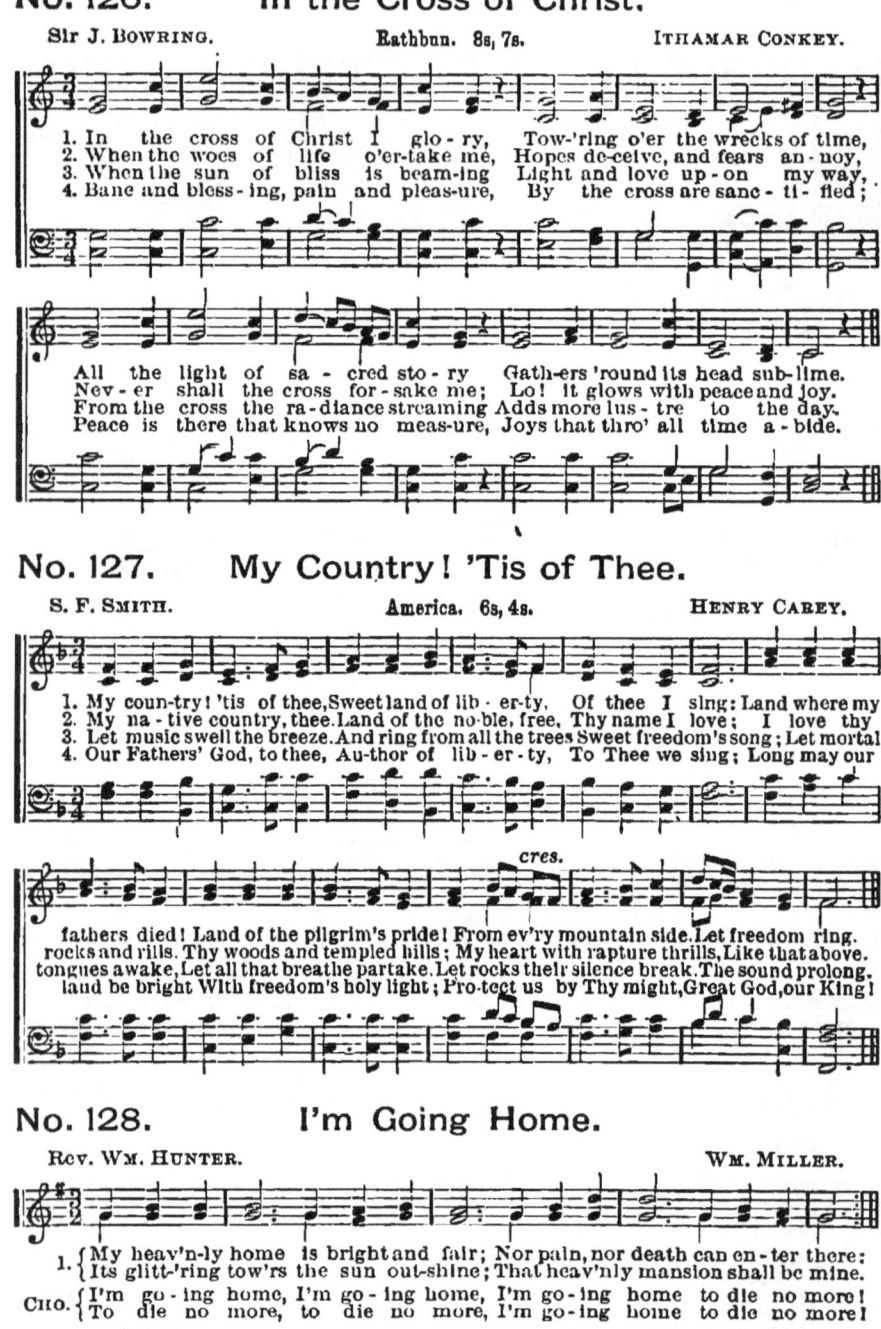

No. 129. My Jesus, as Thou Wilt.

Tr. by Miss J. Borthwick. CARL MARIA VON WEBER.

1. My Jesus, as Thou wilt; O may Thy will be mine; In-to Thy hand of love I would my all re-sign. Thro' sor-row or thro' joy, Conduct me as Thine own, And help me still to say, "My Lord, Thy will be done."

2. My Jesus, as Thou wilt: Tho' seen thro' many a tear, Let not my star of hope Grow dim or dis-ap-pear. Since Thou on earth hast wept And sorrowed oft alone, If I must weep with Thee, "My Lord, Thy will be done."

3. My Jesus, as Thou wilt: All shall be well for me; Each changing fu-ture scene I glad-ly trust with Thee. Straight to my home a-bove, I trav-el calm-ly on, And sing in life or death, "My Lord, Thy will be done."

No. 130. Marching to Zion.

1 Come, we that love the Lord,
  And let our joys be known,
  Join in a song with sweet accord,
  And thus surround the throne.

Cho.—We're marching to Zion,
  Beautiful, beautiful Zion;
  We're marching upward to Zion,
  The beautiful city of God.

2 Let those refuse to sing
  Who never knew our God;
  But children of the heavenly King
  May speak their joys abroad.

3 Then let our song abound,
  And every tear be dry;
  We're marching through Immanuel's
    ground,
  To fairer worlds on high.

No. 131. Come, Ye Sinners.

1 Come, ye sinners, poor and needy,
  Weak and wounded, sick and sore;
  Jesus ready stands to save you,
  Full of pity, love, and power.

Cho—Turn to the Lord, and seek salvation,
  Sound the praise of His dear name;
  Glory, honor, and salvation,
  Christ the Lord has come to reign.

2 Now, ye needy, come and welcome;
  God's free bounty glorify;
  True belief and true repentance,
  Every grace that brings you nigh.

3 Let not conscience make you linger,
  Nor of fitness fondly dream;
  All the fitness He requireth
  Is to feel your need of Him.

No. 132.   O for a Heart to Praise.

CHARLES WESLEY.   THOMAS A. ARNE.

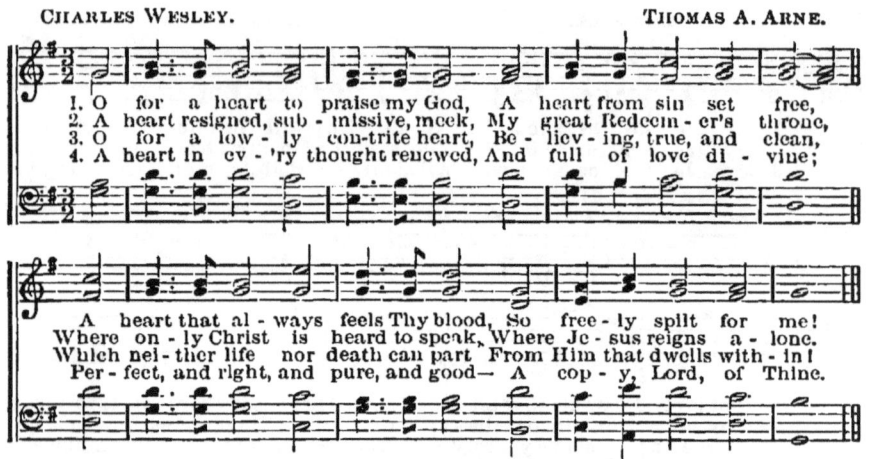

1. O for a heart to praise my God, A heart from sin set free,
2. A heart resigned, sub - missive, meek, My great Redeem - er's throne,
3. O for a low - ly con-trite heart, Be - liev - ing, true, and clean,
4. A heart in ev - 'ry thought renewed, And full of love di - vine;

A heart that al - ways feels Thy blood, So free - ly spilt for me!
Where on - ly Christ is heard to speak, Where Je - sus reigns a - lone.
Which nei - ther life nor death can part From Him that dwells with - in!
Per - fect, and right, and pure, and good— A cop - y, Lord, of Thine.

No. 133.   O for a Faith.   C. M.

1 O for a faith that will not shrink,
    Though pressed by ev'ry foe,
That will not tremble on the brink
    Of any earthly woe!

2 That will not murmur nor complain
    Beneath the chastening rod,
But, in the hour of grief or pain,
    Will lean upon its God;

3 A faith that shines more bright and clear
    When tempests rage without;
That when in danger knows no fear,
    In darkness feels no doubt;

4 Lord, give us such a faith as this;
    And then, whate'er may come,
We'll taste, e'en here, the hallowed bliss
    Of an eternal home.
                   William Hiley Bathurst.

No. 134.   Am I a Soldier.   C. M.

1 Am I a soldier of the cross,
    A foll'wer of the Lamb,
And shall I fear to own His cause,
    Or blush to speak His name?

2 Must I be carried to the skies
    On flowery beds of ease,
While others fought to win the prize,
    And sailed through bloody seas?

3 Are there no foes for me to face?
    Must I not stem the flood?
Is this vile world a friend to grace,
    To help me on to God?

4 Sure I must fight if I would reign;
    Increase my courage, Lord;
I'll bear the toil, endure the pain,
    Supported by Thy word.
                   Isaac Watts.

Azmon.
                                                   C. G. GLASER.

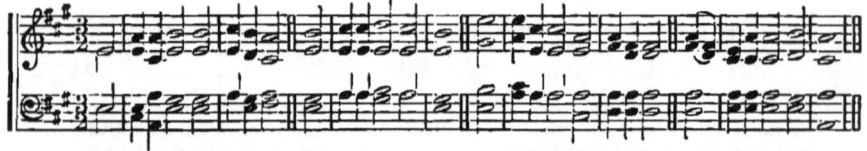

No. 135.   Forever Here My Rest.   C. M.

1 Forever here my rest shall be
    Close to Thy bleeding side;
This all my hope, and all my plea,
    For me the Saviour died.

2 My dying Saviour and my God,
    Fountain for guilt and sin,
Sprinkle me ever with Thy blood,
    And cleanse and keep me clean.

3 Wash me, and make me thus Thine own;
    Wash me, and mine Thou art;
Wash me, but not my feet alone,—
    My hands, my head, my heart.

4 Th' atonement of Thy blood apply,
    Till faith to sight improve;
Till hope in full fruition die,
    And all my soul be love.
                   Charles Wesley.

No. 136.   How Sweet the Name.   C. M.

1 How sweet the name of Jesus sounds
    In a believer's ear!
It soothes his sorrows, heals his wounds,
    And drives away his fear.

2 It makes the wounded spirit whole,
    And calms the troubled breast;
'Tis manna to the troubled soul;
    And to the weary, rest.

3 Dear Name the rock on which I build,
    My shield and hiding-place;
My never-failing treasury, filled
    With boundless stores of grace.

4 Jesus, my Shepherd, Saviour, Friend,
    My Prophet, Priest, and King;
My Lord, my Life, my Way, my End,
    Accept the praise I bring!
                   John Newton.

No. 137. My Jesus, I Love Thee.

London Hymn Book.
A. J. Gordon.

1. My Je-sus, I love Thee, I know Thou art mine, For Thee all the fol-lies of sin I re-sign; My gra-cious Re-deem-er, my Sav-iour art Thou, If ev-er I loved Thee, my Je-sus, 'tis now.
2. I love Thee, because Thou hast first lov-ed me, And purchased my par-don on Cal-va-ry's tree, I love Thee for wear-ing the thorns on Thy brow; If ev-er I loved Thee, my Je-sus, 'tis now.
3. I will love Thee in life, I will love Thee in death, And praise Thee as long as Thou lend-est me breath; And say when the death-dew lies cold on my brow; If ev-er I loved Thee, my Je-sus, 'tis now.
4. In man-sions of glo-ry and end-less de-light, I'll ov-er a-dore Thee in heav-en so bright; I'll sing with the glit-ter-ing crown on my brow; If ev-er I loved Thee, my Je-sus, 'tis now.

Used by permission.

No. 138. There's a Wideness.

Frederick W. Faber.
Lizzie J. Tourjee.

1. There's a wide-ness in God's mer-cy, Like the wide-ness of the sea, There's a kind-ness in His jus-tice, Which is more than lib-er-ty.
2. There is wel-come for the sin-ner, And more gra-ces for the good, There is mer-cy with the Saviour; There is heal-ing in His blood.
3. For the love of God is broad-er Than the meas-ure of man's mind; And the heart of the e-ter-nal, Is most won-der-ful-ly kind.
4. If our love were but more sim-ple, We should take Him at His word; And our lives would be all sun-shine In the sweet-ness of our Lord.

No. 141. Revive Thy Work.

ALBERT MIDLANE.   H. G. NÄGELI.

1. Re-vive Thy work, O Lord, Thy might-y arm make bare;
2. Re-vive Thy work, O Lord, Cre-ate soul-thirst for thee;
3. Re-vive Thy work, O Lord, Ex-alt Thy pre-cious name;

Speak with the voice that wakes the dead, And make Thy peo-ple hear.
And hung-'ring for the Bread of Life, O may our spir-its be!
And by the Ho-ly Ghost, our love For Thee and Thine in-flame.

No. 142.   Blest be the Tie.   S. M.

1 Blest be the tie that binds
   Our hearts in Christian love:
The fellowship of kindred minds
   Is like to that above.

2 Before our Father's throne
   We pour our ardent prayers;
Our fears, our hopes, our aims are one,
   Our comforts and our cares.

3 We share our mutual woes,
   Our mutual burdens bear;
And often for each other flows
   The sympathizing tear.

4 When we asunder part,
   It gives us inward pain;
But we shall still be joined in heart,
   And hope to meet again.

John Fawcett.

No. 143.   A Charge to Keep.

1 A charge to keep I have,
   A God to glorify;
A never-dying soul to save,
   And fit it for the sky.

2 To serve the present age,
   My calling to fulfill,—
Oh, may it all my powers engage,
   To do my Master's will.

3 Arm me with jealous care,
   As in Thy sight to live;
And, oh, Thy servant, Lord, prepare,
   A strict account to give.

4 Help me to watch and pray,
   And on Thyself rely,
Assured, if I my trust betray,
   I shall forever die.

Charles Wesley.

Boylston. S. M.

LOWELL MASON.

No. 144. And Can I Yet Delay. S. M.

1 And can I yet delay
   My little all to give?
To tear my soul from earth away
   For Jesus to receive?

2 Nay, but I yield, I yield!
   I can hold out no more:
I sink, by dying love compelled,
   And own Thee conqueror!

3 Though late, I all forsake;
   My friends, my all resign:
Gracious Redeemer, take, O take,
   And seal me ever Thine.

4 Come, and possess me whole,
   Nor hence again remove:
Settle and fix my wav'ring soul
   With all Thy weight of love.

Charles Wesley.

No. 145. Mourn for the Thousands. S. M.

1 Mourn for the thousands slain,
   The youthful and the strong;
Mourn for the wine cup's fearful reign,
   And the deluded throng.

2 Mourn for the ruined soul—
   Eternal life and light
Lost by the fiery, maddening bowl,
   And turned to hopeless night.

3 Mourn for the lost;—but call,
   Call to the strong, the free;
Rouse them to shun that dreadful fall,
   And to the refuge flee.

4 Mourn for the lost;—but pray,
   Pray to our God above,
To break the fell destroyer's sway,
   And show His saving love.

No. 146. Come, Ye Disconsolate.

THOS. MOORE, alt.
SAMUEL WEBBE.

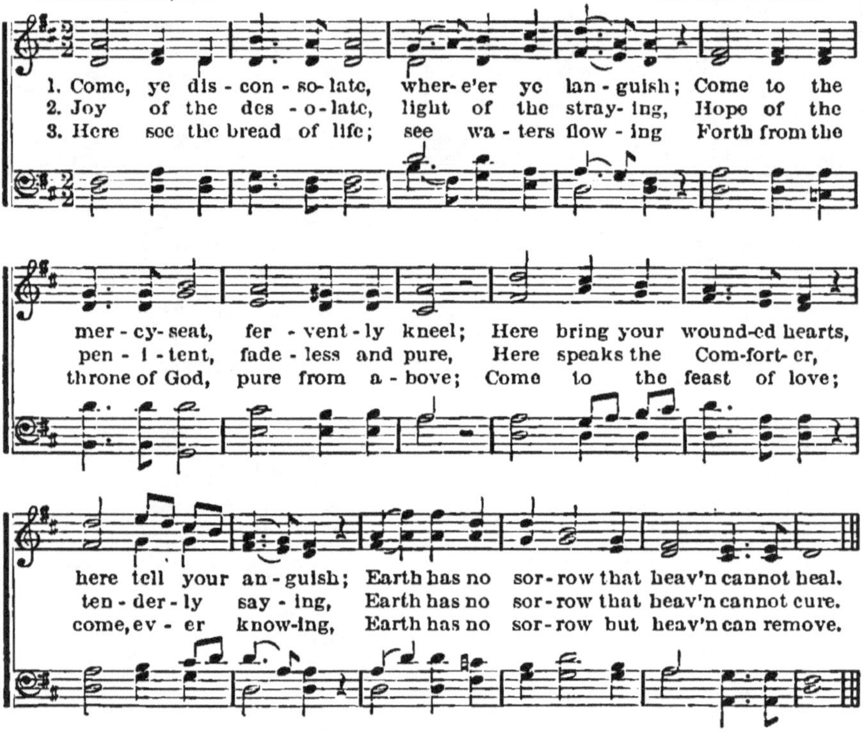

1. Come, ye dis-con-so-late, wher-e'er ye lan-guish; Come to the mer-cy-seat, fer-vent-ly kneel; Here bring your wound-ed hearts, here tell your an-guish; Earth has no sor-row that heav'n cannot heal.
2. Joy of the des-o-late, light of the stray-ing, Hope of the pen-i-tent, fade-less and pure, Here speaks the Com-fort-er, ten-der-ly say-ing, Earth has no sor-row that heav'n cannot cure.
3. Here see the bread of life; see wa-ters flow-ing Forth from the throne of God, pure from a-bove; Come to the feast of love; come, ev-er know-ing, Earth has no sor-row but heav'n can remove.

No. 147. When I Survey the Wondrous Cross.

ISAAC WATTS.
ISAAC BAKER WOODBURY.

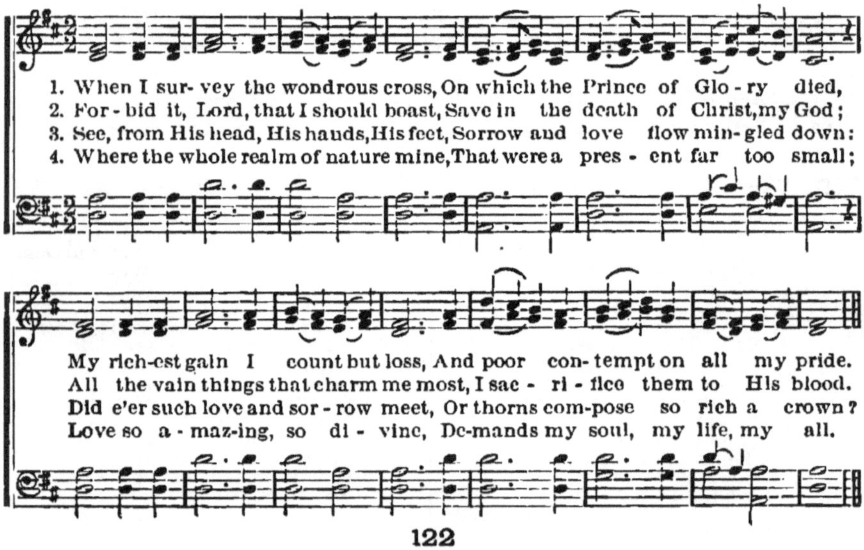

1. When I sur-vey the wondrous cross, On which the Prince of Glo-ry died, My rich-est gain I count but loss, And poor con-tempt on all my pride.
2. For-bid it, Lord, that I should boast, Save in the death of Christ, my God; All the vain things that charm me most, I sac-ri-fice them to His blood.
3. See, from His head, His hands, His feet, Sorrow and love flow min-gled down: Did e'er such love and sor-row meet, Or thorns com-pose so rich a crown?
4. Where the whole realm of nature mine, That were a pres-ent far too small; Love so a-maz-ing, so di-vine, De-mands my soul, my life, my all.

122

No. 148. Walk in the Light.

B. BARTON.   C. M.   From MEHUL and HAYDN.

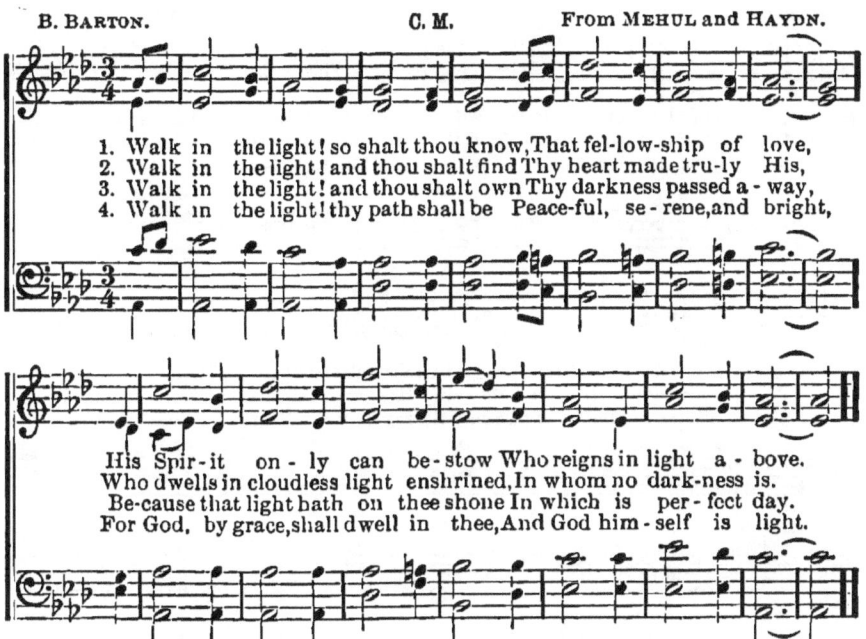

1. Walk in the light! so shalt thou know, That fel-low-ship of love,
His Spir-it on-ly can be-stow Who reigns in light a-bove.
2. Walk in the light! and thou shalt find Thy heart made tru-ly His,
Who dwells in cloudless light enshrined, In whom no dark-ness is.
3. Walk in the light! and thou shalt own Thy darkness passed a-way,
Be-cause that light hath on thee shone In which is per-fect day.
4. Walk in the light! thy path shall be Peace-ful, se-rene, and bright,
For God, by grace, shall dwell in thee, And God him-self is light.

No. 149. O What Amazing Words.

1 O what amazing words of grace
   Are in the gospel found!
Suited to every sinner's case,
   Who knows the joyful sound.

2 Poor, sinful, thirsty, fainting souls
   Are freely welcome here;
Salvation, like a river, rolls
   Abundant, free and clear.

3 Come, then, with all your wants and
   Your every burden bring: [wounds;
Here love, unchanging love, abounds,
   A deep, celestial spring.

4 Millions of sinners, vile as you,
   Have here found life and peace;
Come, then, and prove its virtues too,
   And drink, adore, and bless.
                     S. Medley.

No. 150. When All Thy Mercies.

1 When all Thy mercies, O my God,
   My rising soul surveys,
Transported with the view, I'm lost
   In wonder, love, and praise.

2 O how can words with equal warmth
   The gratitude declare,
That glows within my ravished heart?
   But Thou canst read it there.

3 Through every period of my life
   Thy goodness I'll pursue;
And after death, in distant worlds,
   The pleasing theme renew.

4 Through all eternity to Thee
   A grateful song I'll raise;
But O, eternity's too short
   Too utter all Thy praise.
                     Joseph Addison.

No. 151. Jesus Thine All-Victorious Love.

1 Jesus, thine all-victorious love
   Shed in my heart abroad:
Then shall my feet no longer rove,
   Rooted and fixed in God.

2 O that in me the sacred fire
   Might now begin to glow,
Burn up the dross of base desire
   And make the mountains flow!

3 O that it now from heaven might fall,
   And all my sins consume!
Come, Holy Ghost, for Thee I call;
   Spirit of burning, come!

4 Refining fire, go through my heart;
   Illuminate my soul;
Scatter Thy life through every part,
   And sanctify the whole.
                     C. Wesley.

No. 152. O Could I Speak the Matchless Worth.

SAMUEL MEDLEY.   Arr. by LOWELL MASON.

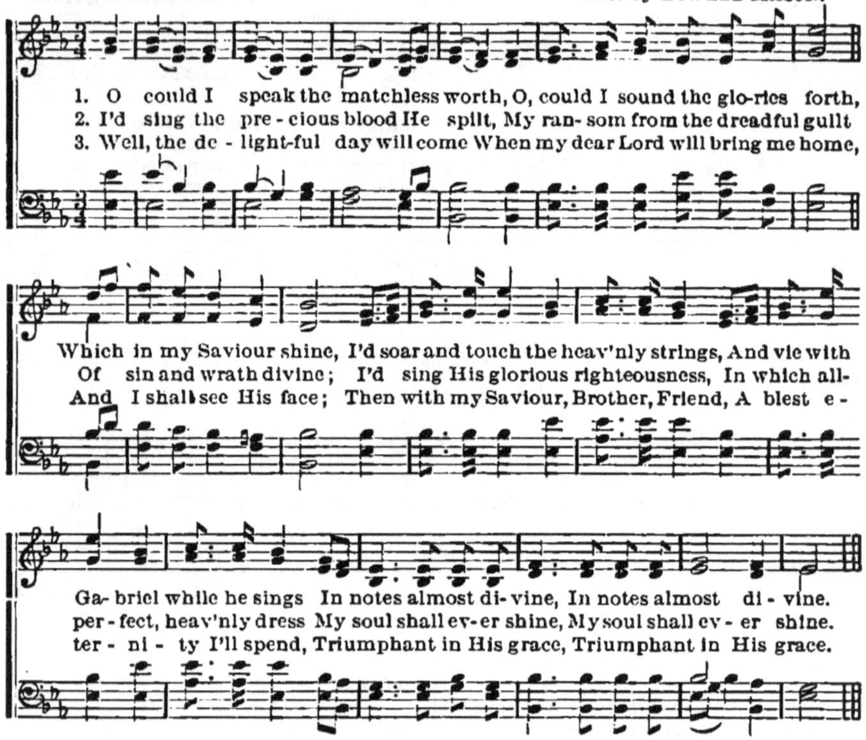

1. O could I speak the matchless worth, O, could I sound the glo-ries forth,
2. I'd sing the pre-cious blood He spilt, My ran-som from the dreadful guilt
3. Well, the de-light-ful day will come When my dear Lord will bring me home,

Which in my Saviour shine, I'd soar and touch the heav'nly strings, And vie with
Of sin and wrath divine; I'd sing His glorious righteousness, In which all-
And I shall see His face; Then with my Saviour, Brother, Friend, A blest e-

Ga-briel while he sings In notes almost di-vine, In notes almost di-vine.
per-fect, heav'nly dress My soul shall ev-er shine, My soul shall ev-er shine.
ter-ni-ty I'll spend, Triumphant in His grace, Triumphant in His grace.

No. 153. I Love Thy Kingdom, Lord.

TIMOTHY DWIGHT.   HANDEL.

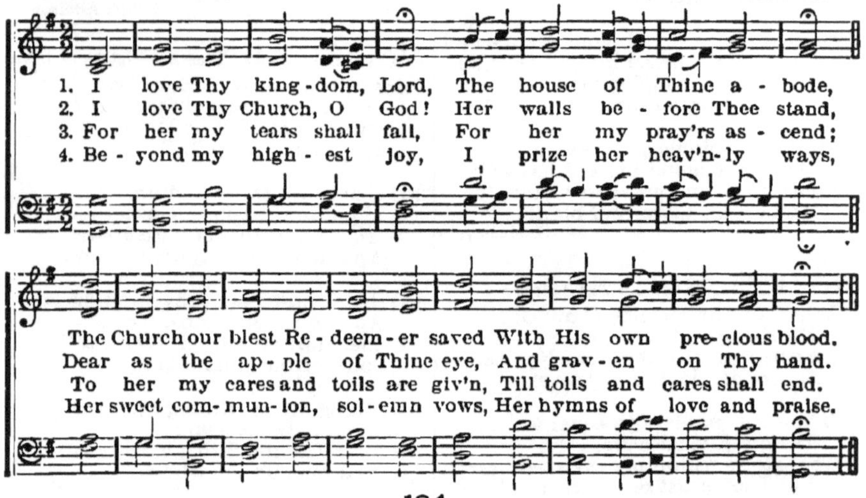

1. I love Thy king-dom, Lord, The house of Thine a-bode,
2. I love Thy Church, O God! Her walls be-fore Thee stand,
3. For her my tears shall fall, For her my pray'rs as-cend;
4. Be-yond my high-est joy, I prize her heav'n-ly ways,

The Church our blest Re-deem-er saved With His own pre-cious blood.
Dear as the ap-ple of Thine eye, And grav-en on Thy hand.
To her my cares and toils are giv'n, Till toils and cares shall end.
Her sweet com-mun-ion, sol-emn vows, Her hymns of love and praise.

No. 156. Stand Up for Jesus.

GEORGE DUFFIELD, Jr. G. J. WEBB.

1. Stand up! stand up for Jesus! Ye soldiers of the cross;
Lift high His royal banner, It must not suffer loss:
D.S.—Till ev'ry foe is vanquished, And Christ is Lord indeed.
From vic-t'ry unto vic-t'ry His army He shall lead,

2 Stand up! stand up for Jesus!
Stand in His strength alone;
The arm of flesh will fail you;
Ye dare not trust your own:
Put on the gospel armor,
And, watching unto prayer,
Where duty calls or danger,
Be never wanting there.

3 Stand up! stand up for Jesus!
The strife will not be long;
This day the noise of battle,
The next the victor's song:
To Him that overcometh,
A crown of life shall be;
He with the King of glory
Shall reign eternally.

No. 157. The Morning Light.

1 The morning light is breaking;
The darkness disappears;
The sons of earth are waking
To penitential tears:
Each breeze that sweeps the ocean
Brings tidings from afar,
Of nations in communion,
Prepared for Zion's war.

2 See heathen nations bending
Before the God we love,
And thousand hearts ascending
In gratitude above;
While sinners, now confessing,
The gospel call obey,
And seek the Saviour's blessing,
A nation in a day.

3 Blest river of salvation,
Pursue thine onward way;
Flow thou to every nation,
Nor in thy richness stay:
Stay not till all the lowly
Triumphant reach their home;
Stay not till all the holy
Proclaim, "The Lord is come!"

Samuel F. Smith.

No. 158. Praise God.

THOMAS KEN. Old Hundred. L. M. LOUIS BOURGEOIS.

Praise God, from whom all blessings flow; Praise Him, all creatures here below;
Praise Him above, ye heav'nly host; Praise Father, Son, and Holy Ghost.

www.ingramcontent.com/pod-product-compliance
Lightning Source LLC
Chambersburg PA
CBHW031343160426
43196CB00007B/720